WORDS
THAT
MATTER

WORDS THAT MATTER

* *A* Little Book *of* Life Lessons *

FROM THE EDITORS OF

O, THE OPRAH MAGAZINE

harperstudio
An Imprint of HarperCollins*Publishers*

O, The Oprah Magazine
Founder and Editorial Director: Oprah Winfrey
Editor in Chief: Susan Casey
Editor at Large: Gayle King

Contributors
Editor: Michelle Burford
Associate Editor: Dorothea Hunter

HarperCollins books may be purchased for educational, business, or sales promotional use. For information please write: Special Markets Department, HarperCollins Publishers, 10 East 53rd Street, New York, NY 10022.

For more information about this book or other books from Harper Studio, visit www.theharperstudio.com.

FIRST EDITION

Library of Congress Cataloging-in-Publication Data

  Words that matter : a little book of life lessons / by editors of O, the Oprah magazine.
    p. cm.
  ISBN 978-0-06-199633-7
  1. Conduct of life—Quotations, maxims, etc.
BJ1581.2.W678 2010
170'.44—dc22

                                                      2010004096

10 11 12 13 14 ID/RRD   10 9 8 7 6 5 4 3 2 1

CONTENTS

FOREWORD

✳

I've lived my life by quotations and sayings. Even as a girl, I memorized phrases like "Excellence is the best deterrent to racism and sexism, so be excellent," a line I first heard from the Reverend Jesse Jackson at a high-school assembly. Since then, I've Scotch-taped dozens of other one-liners to my mirrors and walls—from poet Alexander Pope's "Blessed is he who expects nothing, for he shall never be disappointed" to my favorite quotation of Dr. Martin Luther King Jr.: "Everyone has the power for greatness, not for fame, but greatness, because greatness is determined by service." Over the years, as I've taken on new challenges, I've used these words as a guiding principle.

I created a magazine because I wanted you to be as transformed as I've been by the written word—to live a life that's as meaningful, vibrant, intentional, and, yes, even as pleasurable as it can possibly be. This book holds some of my favorite words of wisdom, which I've gathered over the last decade. In these pages, you'll find a treasure trove of advice, humor, motivation, and encouragement—gems of truth on subjects ranging from dreaming big and aging brilliantly to strengthening your connections with loved ones, nurturing your spiritual self, and blowing the lid off whatever box you're stuck in. Yes, my editors and I have included some of the most thought-provoking quotations. For example, this one from British novelist Jeanette Winterson: "There is no discovery without risk—and what you risk reveals what you value." But we've also sprinkled in plenty of frivolity and fun, like Bette Midler's "We're all divine, but I was the only one who had the nerve to call myself that. And I thought of it first. So there!"

I hope this little volume will become a staple that resides on your nightstand or that you throw in your tote to inspire you wherever you go. When you catch yourself dreaming too small, battling discouragement, lacking joy, or sliding off balance, crack it open. Here's what my love affair with quotations has taught me: the more you focus on words that uplift you, the more you embody the ideas contained in those words.

I love the way Ralph Waldo Emerson once put it: "We become what we think about all day long."

Everything you and I experience—be it a valley or a victory, a crisis or a Kilimanjaro moment—contains a seed of grace, a lesson for the journey ahead. As you courageously navigate your own path, consider the purchase of this little book of life lessons a gift to yourself, a gathering of some delightful aha's and lightbulb moments that others have been gracious enough to pass on. Savor them. Share them. And whenever you need a pick-me-up or a bolt of inspiration, return to them.

Oprah Winfrey

WORDS
THAT
MATTER

DREAMING BIG,
BECOMING BRAVE

✳

IT'S ONLY WHEN YOU MAKE THE
PROCESS YOUR GOAL THAT THE BIG
DREAM CAN FOLLOW.

—OPRAH

"As long as we dare to dream and don't get in the way of ourselves, anything is possible—there's truly no end to where our dreams can take us." —*Hilary Swank, actress*

"Be daring, be different, be anything that will assert integrity of purpose and imaginative vision against the play-it-safers . . ."
—*Cecil Beaton, photographer*

"Years ago I was in the parking lot across the street from Spago, I could see the stars with their Oscars going into the after party. I said to myself, 'I want to do that one day' . . . After I got the Oscar and walked offstage, I said to Kevin [Kline], 'Did that just happen?' It felt like I fell asleep in the mail room and I was going to wake up and find out it was all a dream."
—*Denzel Washington, actor*

"My mother and father were poor, and when I turned pro, I started making money . . . I wasn't thinking of being the greatest. But I knew I had a chance. And when I won at the Olympics, that sealed it: I was the champ." —*Muhammad Ali, former heavyweight champion boxer*

"Nothing really worth having is easy to get. The hard-fought battles, the goals won with sacrifice, are the ones that matter."
—*Aisha Tyler, actress and comedian*

"Fortune helps those who dare." —*Virgil, poet*

"Imagination is the beginning of creation. You imagine what you desire, you will what you imagine, and at last you create what you will." —*George Bernard Shaw, playwright*

"I fear only God. I don't fear any human. When you have that kind of spirit, you can just do what you have to do. Let it roll."
—*Stevie Wonder, singer*

"My life . . . is about not knowing, having to change, taking the moment and making the best of it, without knowing what's going to happen next." —*Gilda Radner, actress*

"If you can allow yourself to breathe into the depth, wonder, beauty, craziness, and strife—everything that represents the fullness of your life—you can live fearlessly. Because you come to realize that if you just keep breathing, you cannot be conquered." —*Oprah*

"One night a seventy-year-old woman came up to me after the show [*The Color Purple* on Broadway] and told me she'd also been a single mother who had dropped out of school, and now she's taking nursing classes. She said, 'You inspired me.' You can't tell me that dreams don't come true. My life is proof that they do." —*Fantasia Barrino*, American Idol *winner*

"Living is a form of not being sure, not knowing what next or how . . . We guess. We may be wrong, but we take leap after leap in the dark." —*Agnes de Mille, dancer*

"Adventure comes with no guarantees or promises. Risk and reward are conjoined twins—and that's why my favorite piece of advice needs translation but no disclaimers: *Fortes fortuna javat*. 'Fortune favors the brave,' the ancient Roman dramatist Terence declared. In other words, there are many good reasons not to toss your life up in the air and see where it lands. Just don't let fear be one of them." —*Mary South, author*

"I come from a family whose belief was, You can do it, but you have to work really hard." —*Condoleeza Rice, former U.S. secretary of state*

"There are so many talented actors who don't ever get the chance . . . I go down on my knees in extreme gratitude. I don't take it for granted. I know all these actors who are probably more talented than I am. I've taken the chance and done my best with it." —*Charlize Theron, actress*

"Failure is a signpost to turn you in another direction." —*Oprah*

"The people who get on in this world are the people who get up and look for the circumstances they want, and, if they can't find them, make them." —*George Bernard Shaw, playwright*

"You can do anything you want to do. What is rare is this actual wanting to do a certain thing: wanting it so much that you are practically blind to other things, that nothing else will satisfy you . . . I know I have said a lot when I say, 'You can do anything you want to do.' But I mean it . . . Blunder ahead with your personal view . . . The real work of art is the result of a magnificent struggle." —*Robert Henri, painter*

"What I know for sure is that no matter where you stand right now—on a hilltop, in a gutter, at a crossroads, in a rut—you need to give yourself the best you have to offer in this moment. This is it. Rather than depleting yourself with judgments about what you haven't done, who you could have become, why you haven't moved faster, or what you should have changed, redirect that energy toward the next big push—the one that takes you from enough to better. The one that takes you from adequate to extraordinary. The one that helps you rise up from a low moment and reach for your personal best." —*Oprah*

"Dreams come true; without that possibility, nature would not incite us to have them." —*John Updike, author*

"In action lies wisdom and confidence."
—*Albert Schweitzer, theologian*

"To be fully human is . . . to know that it's possible to face the unimaginable and somehow put one foot in front of the other."
—*Oprah*

"To follow your life's guidance, you may have to reassign some seemingly important things to 'unimportant.' If you believe that pleasing your horrible boss or having a spotless house is a higher priority than playing with your children or sleeping off the flu, be prepared for a long and strenuous battle against destiny. Also, be prepared to lose." —*Martha Beck, life coach*

"Miracles sometimes happen, but more often they're made of faith and wit and hope and imagination, to say nothing of sweat." —*Tom Waldman, writer*

"When people tell me something is impossible, I try to prove them wrong." —*Richard Branson, entrepreneur*

"I have learned over the years that when one's mind is made up, this diminishes fear; knowing what must be done does away with fear." —*Rosa Parks, civil rights pioneer*

"Life shrinks or expands in proportion to one's courage."
—*Anaïs Nin, author*

"You gain strength, courage, and confidence by every experience in which you really stop to look fear in the face . . . You must do the thing you think you cannot do."
—*Eleanor Roosevelt, former First Lady*

"I truly believe that a woman can have anything she wants—if she's willing to do the hard work it takes to get it." —*Oprah*

"The only courage that matters is the kind that gets you from one moment to the next." —*Mignon McLaughlin, journalist*

"Courage is only an accumulation of small steps."
—*George Konrad, author*

"A voice in me said, You have to rise to the occasion or the best in you will die. We always have that voice; we just have to make a choice to listen to it. We all have it; that's God's given light. It's just whether you have the courage to step into your destiny." —*Lily Yeh, artist*

"I believe that one of life's greatest risks is never daring to risk . . . Do the one thing you think you cannot do. Fail at it. Try again. Do better the second time. The only people who never tumble are those who never mount the high wire." —*Oprah*

"One of the things that's great about failure is, it's never as bad as you think it's going to be. You think it's going to be the end of the world, and it's really not." —*Lisa Rau, writer*

"I notice well that one stray step from the habitual path leads irresistibly into a new direction." —*Franz Grillparzer, playwright and poet*

"What would happen if we declared our home, our relationships, our lives a gossip-free zone? We'd probably be surprised at how much time we'd free up to do the work that's most significant—building our dreams rather than tearing down others'." —*Oprah*

"Courage is the most important of all virtues, because without courage, you cannot practice any of the other virtues consistently." —*Maya Angelou, author*

"Every successful person I have ever known has had it—that instinct to sense and seize the right moment without wavering or playing it safe." —*Moss Hart, playwright*

"Success is a journey, not a destination. The doing is often more important than the outcome." —*Arthur Ashe, tennis champion*

"All of us need a vision for our lives, and even as we work to achieve that vision, we must surrender to the power that is greater than we know. It's one of the defining principles of my life that I love to share: God can dream a bigger dream for you than you could ever dream for yourself." —*Oprah*

"You need more than just passion to start a business—you need a plan." —*Suze Orman, finance expert*

"The only courage you ever need is the courage to live your heart's desire." —*Oprah*

"First say to yourself what you would be; and then do what you have to do." —*Epictetus, philosopher*

"Nothing great in the world has been accomplished without passion." —*Georg Wilhelm Friedrich Hegel, philosopher*

"To fulfill a dream, to be allowed to sweat over lonely labor, to be given the chance to create, is the meat and potatoes of life." —*Bette Davis, actress*

"There is only one success . . . to be able to spend your life in your own way." —*Christopher Morley, author and journalist*

"I began to develop a very focused sense of purpose when I was about twenty. That's when the Islamic Revolution turned my world upside down. I lost friends and family, my home and possessions. The revolution propelled me to where I am today: trying to make sense of our world. My commitment is to constancy . . . I have not changed what I believe about truth, integrity, morality, and duty." —*Christiane Amanpour, international correspondent*

"I think we're shaped by failure at least as much as we're shaped by our successes. When I have guests on a show, I like to talk to them about their failures—not to show them up, but because that's part of what defines us. Sometimes it's not the cheery, upbeat lessons that really explain how a person got to be where they are. It's the things they tried to do and couldn't do. The things they're still struggling to do." —*Terry Gross, radio program host*

"Try more things. Learning to swim won't stop you from reading Shakespeare. Finding your voice won't stop you from writing novels. You should be cooking on all four burners." —*Breena Clarke, novelist*

"The only place where success comes before work is a dictionary." —*Vidal Sassoon, hair-care entrepreneur*

"As much as you plan and dream and move forward in your life, you must remember that you are always acting in conjunction with the flow and energy of the universe. You move in the direction of your goal with all the force and verve you can muster—and then let go, releasing your plan to the power that's bigger than yourself . . . Dream big—dream very big. Work hard—work very hard. And after you've done all you can, you stand, wait, and fully surrender." —*Oprah*

"The person with the plan most often carries the day." —*Phil McGraw, psychologist*

"I do have a core of trust that I'll figure things out and find my way. And if whatever I try is not a good experience, even that is a good experience. If something turns out badly, it's interesting." —*Julie Taymor, theater director*

"God doesn't require us to succeed; he only requires that you try." —*Mother Teresa, Catholic nun and Nobel Peace Prize recipient*

"Courage means doing the impossible within the possible." —*Elie Wiesel, Holocaust survivor and Nobel Peace Prize recipient*

"Let passion drive your profession." —*Oprah*

"Success is relative. It is what we can make of the mess we have made of things." —*T. S. Eliot, poet and playwright*

"Hope begins in the dark, the stubborn hope that if you just show up and try to do the right thing, the dawn will come. You wait and watch and work. You don't give up."
—*Anne Lamott, writer*

"There's an old gospel song with a refrain I love: 'I've got fire, fire, fire shut up in my bones.' We were all born with this fire, but beginning in childhood, we let others snuff it out. Passion is the log that keeps the fire of purpose blazing. Your work now is to find that fire and rekindle it—and then let it burn."
—*Oprah*

"We are more than we imagine ourselves to be. It's what we tell our children, our parents, our friends. But how often do we tell it to ourselves? And if we do, how often do we prove it? How often do we challenge ourselves to do something new?"
—*Veronica Chambers, author and journalist*

"It's only when we truly know that we have a limited time on earth—and that we have no way of knowing when our time is up—that we will begin to live each day to the fullest, as if it [were] the only one we had." —*Elisabeth Kübler-Ross, psychiatrist*

"My only guiding light has been my desire to be the best actor I can be, no matter how daunting the process. I still have to squeeze my way into auditions, because people can't imagine that someone who looks the way I do could play a certain role. It doesn't occur to them—but I know I can make it occur to them, if they just give me a chance."
—*Sandra Oh, actress*

"Whether you believe you can do a thing or not, you are right."
—*Henry Ford, auto company founder*

"Success is liking yourself, liking what you do, and liking how you do it." —*Maya Angelou, author*

"Change is the only constant; hanging on is the only sin."
—*Denise McCluggage, race car driver*

"Destiny is not a matter of chance, it is a matter of choice; it is not a thing to be waited for, it's a thing to be achieved."
—*William Jennings Bryan, politician and statesman*

"It's really not just one choice that matters—it's all the baby choices that will lead you to the ultimate moment, when you can make the strongest stand and commitment to yourself and the life that's calling you." —*Oprah*

"Success is to be measured not so much by the position that one has reached in life as by the obstacles which he has overcome."
—*Booker T. Washington, political leader and author*

"I cannot give you the formula for success, but I can give you the formula for failure, which is: Try to please everybody."
—*Herbert Bayard Swope, journalist*

"There are no secrets to success. It is a result of preparation, hard work, and learning from failure." —*Colin Powell, former U.S. secretary of state*

"The true meaning of courage is to be afraid, and then, with your knees knocking and your heart racing, to step out anyway—even when that step makes sense to nobody but you. I know that's not easy. But making a bold move is the only way to truly advance toward the grandest vision the universe has for you." —*Oprah*

"There is a strength and spirit in Americans that is rare and unparalleled anywhere in the world. We have a resilience that most people don't have, and trials bring out the best in us."
—*Madeleine Albright, former U.S. secretary of state*

"Even the most powerful women I know go out of their way to say that they're not really interested in power. Imagine a man saying that." —*Susan Estrich, lawyer*

"If you have an impulse to do something, and it's not totally irresponsible, why not do it? It might be just the journey you've always needed." —*Timothy Hutton, actor*

"I have never encountered a successful person who didn't have to sacrifice in one area of life in order to be successful in another . . . If you have tons of resources in the monetary account but zero balances in the emotional, family, physical, and spiritual accounts, that spells a bankrupt life." —*Phil McGraw, psychologist*

"I like to dream big! Education is the key to unlocking the world, a passport to freedom—and to the children of Africa, education is everything. So it's with tremendous pleasure that I introduce you to my dreams come true: the girls who will grow up to be the women who will be the leaders of tomorrow." —*Oprah*

"If life doesn't offer you a game worth playing, then invent a new one." —*Anthony J. D'Angelo, author*

"I've never done anything for the sake of ambition that I regret . . . Ambition can look very good on some women. If you find the world hates you for it, then sure, stop raising your hand in class—but be sure to get the A anyway." —*Joni Evans, literary agent*

"I think people who lack self-esteem lack it because they haven't taken enough risks and haven't succeeded enough. Nobody can talk you into feeling good about yourself—you get the solid good feelings from success." —*David K. Reynolds, psychotherapist*

"Before opening your mouth, ask yourself two questions: What do I really want? Is what I'm about to say or do right now going to get me closer to what I want?"—*Terrence Real, relationship coach*

"My definition of possible has broadened remarkably, as has my ability to pursue those possibilities with calm assurance. In the past, I thought I could only bring one thing to the world, but now the world is welcoming me in other ways. My career is fulfilling, but so is finding a stray cat a loving home." —*Stacey Grenrock-Woods, television comedy writer*

"I believe that if you'll just stand up and go, life will open up for you."—*Tina Turner, singer*

"*Surviving* is unrelenting perseverance that brings us back to where we were before our crisis. *Thriving* is a kind of superresilience that goes far beyond recovery. Thrivers know when it's time to disengage from a challenge and set new goals. Sometimes creative surrender is a better policy than perseverance."
—*Paul Pearsall, psychologist*

※

"FOR ME, THE PATH TO SUCCESS WAS NEVER ABOUT ATTAINING INCREDIBLE WEALTH OR CELEBRITY. IT WAS ABOUT THE PROCESS OF CONTINUALLY SEEKING TO BE BETTER, TO CHALLENGE MYSELF TO PURSUE EXCELLENCE ON EVERY LEVEL. THE QUESTION I ASK EVERY DAY IS THE SAME AS IT'S ALWAYS BEEN: HOW MUCH FARTHER CAN I STRETCH TO REACH MY FULL POTENTIAL? WHAT I KNOW FOR SURE IS THAT IT'S ONLY WHEN YOU MAKE THE *PROCESS* YOUR GOAL THAT THE DREAM CAN FOLLOW."
—OPRAH

CONNECTING: LOVE, SEX, FRIENDSHIP, AND FAMILY

THE CHANCE TO LOVE AND BE LOVED
EXISTS NO MATTER WHERE YOU ARE.

—OPRAH

"All intimacy is rare—that's what makes it precious. And it involves the revelation of one's self and the loving gaze upon another's true self (no makeup, no fancy car, no defensive charm, no seduction)—that's what makes it so damn hard. Intimacy requires honesty and kindness in almost equal measure (a little more kindness, I think), trust and trustworthiness, forgiveness and the capacity to be forgiven . . . It's more than worth it—just don't let them tell you it's bliss." —*Amy Bloom, author*

"The love of our neighbor in all its fullness simply means being able to say to him, 'What are you going through?'"
—*Simone Weil, philosopher*

"To know that people care about how you're doing when the doings aren't so good—that's what love is." —*Oprah*

"I've never been without friends. Never. I've never not had a best girlfriend. I can go through their names from the time I was five years old: Betty, Charlotte, Sylvia . . . I can't understand women living without women friends. I don't know how they do it." —*Genine Lentine, poet*

"A man will feel even more motivated to please a woman he loves if he knows that, in general, she already thinks the world of him." —*Jay Carter, psychologist*

"I know it's said you should love yourself before you can be in a relationship, but hell, I did it backward." —*Jennifer Aniston, actress*

"We've got this gift of love, but love is like a precious plant . . . You've got to keep watering it. You've got to really look after it and nurture it." —*John Lennon, singer*

"Being a good husband is like being a good stand-up comic—you need ten years before you can even call yourself a beginner." —*Jerry Seinfeld, comedian*

"There are a lot of little divorces that have to occur for a good marriage to last. Barbie Doll and Fantasizing Hubby didn't last. We did because we were able to discard them." —*Julia Alvarez, author*

"If you're telling yourself that you're the greatest thing since the iPod but deep down inside you believe you are an eight-track player or the 'chubby girl' who couldn't catch a man with a net and a pack of hunting dogs, then you're heading for more nights alone than a cloistered nun." —*Phil McGraw, psychologist*

"It's simple: When you haven't forgiven those who've hurt you, you turn your back against your future. When you do forgive, you start walking forward." —*Tyler Perry, director*

"Some desire DiCaprio, others crave Clooney, I have a little thing for Desmond Tutu, or as I like to call him, Archbishop McDreamy. What can I tell you? I've always been a sucker for integrity and twinkly eyes." —*Lisa Kogan, writer*

"I had latched onto domesticity to fill the holes in my relationship. I couldn't connect emotionally with my husband, but I could feed him. I could not make him love me more or better, but I could cook and clean and decorate . . . In time these choices made me tight and joyless, as I fretted about thread counts and piecrusts and all manner of things that did not bring us an inch closer . . . After eight years of marriage, it was exhilarating to break free of the need to accommodate."
—*Allison Glock, writer*

"This is a deep, permanent human condition, this need to be loved and to love." —*Annie Proulx, writer*

"To actually have sex, I must be not only in love but also in full legal possession of the other party's medical records. The advantage of this approach is that what you miss in casual thrills, you gain in long-term compatibility. That initial spark of interest leads not only to the nearest motel room but to the prolonged scrutiny you would give an unrecognizable substance before deciding to include it in a cake."
—*Martha Beck, life coach*

"Love yourself and then learn to extend that love to others in every encounter." —*Oprah*

"We've got a budget deficit that's important, we've got a trade deficit that's critical, but what I worry about most is our empathy deficit. When I speak to students, I tell them that one of the most important things we can do is to look through somebody else's eyes." —*Barack Obama, president of the United States*

"Oxytocin is a brain chemical that produces feelings of trust and attachment. Men get a blast of it when they kiss, women feel a rush when they hold a lover's hand, and during orgasm, both partners are flooded with the powerful substance . . . enjoy each other physically. Good sex really does build intimacy." —*Helen Fisher, anthropologist*

"The roses, the lovely notes, the dining and dancing are all welcome and splendid. But when the Godiva is gone the gift of real love is having someone who'll go the distance with you. Someone who, when the wedding day limo breaks down, is willing to share a seat on the bus." —*Oprah*

"It takes something to get married: nerve, hope, a strong desire to make a certain statement—and it takes something to stay married: more hope, determination, a sense of humor, and needs that are best met by being in a pair." —*Amy Bloom, writer*

"The moment we begin tolerating meanness, in ourselves and others, we are using our authorial power in the service of wrongdoing. We have both the capacity and the obligation to do better." —*Martha Beck, life coach*

"As a man, it can be confusing to know what role to play. There I was, with the woman I would soon marry, trying to jockey for position in her life. What did it mean to be her significant other? . . . It meant that I needed to hear her when she spoke to me. Trying to come up with ways to solve her problems gave me a false sense of control, and when I offered up unsolicited advice, I was disrespecting a strong woman who knew how to handle her own life." —*Blair Underwood, actor*

"I've always known that life is better when you share it. I now realize it gets even sweeter when you expand the circle." —*Oprah*

"Good sex, healthy sex, is a kind of play. Be willing to get good at it, and find out what it's going to take for you to like and accept yourself. Know what makes you happy sexually. Acknowledge the power you have as a woman. Then give yourself permission to be sexual and enjoy it." —*Phil McGraw, psychologist*

"People can love more than once. And love happens to people of all ages, because one's internal life changes, as well as one's opportunities. I don't see love as something that if you don't get it by the time you're thirty, cross it off the list."
—*Ethel Person, medical doctor and psychoanalyst*

"At its best, highest form, charm is a show of generosity and moral goodness, an extension of the self toward others that permits them to shine. By helping others relax and unfold, charm allows you to shine, too. Unlike any other quality I can think of, it's self-effacing, self-protective, and attention-getting at the same time." —*Peter Smith, writer*

"In a true partnership, the kind worth striving for, the kind worth insisting on, and even, frankly, worth divorcing over, both people try to give as much or even a little more than they get. 'Deserves' is not the point. And 'owes' is certainly not the point. The point is to make the other person as happy as we can, because their happiness adds to ours. The point is—in the right hands, everything that you give, you get."
—*Amy Bloom, writer*

"Being a mother is the hardest job on earth. Women everywhere must declare it so." —*Oprah*

"Every aspect of marriage has to be negotiated: You must reach a comfortable agreement on sex, religion, finances, division of labor—just to name a few issues . . . Claim your rights. Do so with sensitivity, but claim them nonetheless."
—*Phil McGraw, psychologist*

"In love, one and one are one."
—*Jean-Paul Sartre, philosopher*

"He has achieved success, who has lived well, laughed often, and loved much." —*Bessie A. Stanley, poet*

"People should not judge failed love affairs as failed experiences but as part of the growth process. Something does not have to end well for it to have been one of the most valuable experiences of a lifetime." —*Ethel Person, medical doctor and psychoanalyst*

"Having a mate is like holding a mirror up to yourself. You see both how good you look and how much emotional surgery is required. That's the way it's supposed to be. The fairy-tale notion of happily-ever-after that we've all bought into is indeed a tale and nothing like real love." —*Oprah*

"If I had to choose between someone there at home who celebrates with you but who also criticizes you, and being alone, I'd rather be alone, keep my good friends, and have my freedom." —*Wanda Sykes, comedian*

"If you want to capture people's attention, put your own attention on something that has nothing to do with them: oil painting, cooking, wildlife rescue. The more you get lost in what you're doing, the more interesting you'll become."
—*Martha Beck, life coach*

"I believe that love expands. As you give love out, it's received and reciprocated—and it grows. That's the beauty of it. Love is an energy. You can feed it to people, and they in turn feed it to others, and eventually it comes back." —*Hill Harper, actor*

"Wherever groups of women make connections with other groups of women . . . we are affirming a network of change."
—*Blanche Welsen Cook, writer*

"Be courteous to all but intimate with few; and let those few be well tried before you give them your confidence."
—*George Washington, first president of the United States*

"We must decide what we need love to be. Ginger Rogers and Fred Astaire offer no insight for me. The chronically healthy can live that 1930s Hollywood version of perfect love. The physically flawed cannot. The whole person must be more than the sum of flawed parts." —*Richard M. Cohen, journalist*

"Love was once associated with joy, fun, and happiness, and it would be nice if it were so again." —*James Collins, writer*

"What my generation was raised to believe—that people get married and stay together because they love each other—is no longer the whole truth. Only when love is a verb and put into action does it thrive. It's a mistake to think that a loving relationship is going to automatically sustain itself. Nothing worth having happens without work." —*Oprah*

"Know yourself and know your family. For me, that means knowing that, as much as I appreciated my mother's sweetness and practical ways, I need a slightly reckless lion more than I need a sensible lamb in my life . . . I married a lion, and although I never pictured myself being the person hanging on to the 'oh shit' bar on the passenger side, saying, 'For God's sake, honey, slow down!' I do prefer that to being the person who says, regularly, 'Honey, if you're scared, we can turn around.'" —*Amy Bloom, writer*

"Love is everything it's cracked up to be . . . It really is worth fighting for, being brave for, risking everything for."
—*Erica Jong, author*

"You shower regularly, right? Something as important as the physical intimacy of a relationship deserves at least as much emphasis as a shower! . . . Carve out time for lovemaking. Yes, it takes away spontaneity when you have to pencil in sex, but at least you'll be having it!" —*Phil McGraw, psychologist*

"I think romantic love is one of the great change agents. We come to know ourselves in a different way when we fall in love, and whatever happens to that relationship, we are changed. We know something we didn't know before. We discover capacities that we didn't know we had." —*Ethel Person, medical doctor and psychoanalyst*

"Detached, genuine interest in another person's inner experience is, if anything, more seductive than the hair flips I will never master." —*Martha Beck, life coach*

"Two years ought to be long enough to figure out whether you want somebody to be your life partner. My theory has always been if it takes a person that long to talk himself into something, then it's not right." —*Phil McGraw, psychologist*

"What else is love but understanding and rejoicing in the fact that another person lives, acts, and experiences otherwise than we do . . . ?" —*Friedrich Nietzsche, philosopher*

"Plans frequently fail and dreams have been known to dim. But come the morning, there are your friends offering sweet salvation and good gossip and the occasional glass of sauvignon blanc with lunch. If ever there was a reason for hope, I think maybe that's it." —*Lisa Kogan, writer*

"Nothing guarantees a long and happy marriage except two people willing to throw themselves, headlong, into the uncertainty, the inevitable pain and disappointment, the absolutely guaranteed failures and essential bravery, of intimacy. It does take two—and that's a shame, because so many not-too-bad marriages have one person who is willing to make that leap and one who is, at heart, not—but if you have two people who are willing to make themselves better, more vulnerable, more honest than they were the year before, you, you lucky few, have a shot at the long and happy." —*Amy Bloom, author*

"To love and be loved is to feel the sun from both sides." —*David Viscott, psychiatrist*

"Change from a critical habit of mind, in which you're very involved with your partner's mistakes, to a positive one, in which you catch him doing something right." —*John Gottman, psychologist*

"I know for sure that in the final analysis of our lives—when the to-do lists are no more, when the frenzy is finished, when our e-mail boxes are empty—the only thing that will have any lasting value is whether we've loved others and whether they've loved us." —*Oprah*

"Love is, above all else, the gift of oneself." —*Jean Anouilh, playwright*

"Here's a phrase that must never, ever cross your lips: 'Let me tell you why a terrific gal like you is still single . . .' Because that terrific gal is then likely to explain in dark and visceral detail what happened to the last gentleman who uttered those very words—and, trust me, you really don't want to know." —*Lisa Kogan, writer*

"The married are those who have taken the terrible risk of intimacy, and, having taken it, know life without intimacy to be impossible." —*Carolyn Heilbrun, author*

"Intimacy requires courage because risk is inescapable."
—*Rollo May, psychologist*

"None of us seems to accept that we are incredibly precious—that when I dehumanize you, I am dehumanized . . . God's dream is that we could know that we are members of one family. There are no outsiders—black, white, rich, poor, male, female, gay, lesbian, and so-called straight. Bin Laden. Bush. Sharon. They all belong." —*Desmond Tutu, Anglican archbishop*

"If you are in love . . . that's about the best thing that can happen to anyone. Don't let anyone make it small or light to you."
—*John Steinbeck, author*

"Love is that splendid triggering of human vitality . . . the supreme activity which nature affords anyone for going out of himself toward someone else." —*José Ortega y Gasset, philosopher*

"For two people to be happy together, they have to feel that their needs are being met. But there's not a soul on earth who can meet your needs if you don't even know what they are. You've got to do some self-exploration so that you know firmly who you are, what you value, and what will fulfill you."
—*Phil McGraw, psychologist*

"Our capacity to love often depends on having a good child-hood—not a great one, just good enough." —*Ethel Person, medical doctor and psychoanalyst*

"Loneliness, far from revealing some defect, is proof that your innate search for connection is intact. So instead of hiding your loneliness, bring it into the light. Honor it. Treat it. Heal it. You'll find that it returns the favor." —*Martha Beck, life coach*

"I now know that a relationship built on real love feels good. It isn't selfish; it doesn't cause you anxiety. When someone really loves you, he understands that you're lovable just because you're here. How he treats you underscores that understanding." —*Oprah*

"Loving can cost a lot, but not loving always costs more." —*Merle Shain, journalist*

"I've left a couple of husbands, and here's what I've learned: If you cannot support yourself, you set yourself up to be a prisoner. We can't stay home like June Cleaver and expect a man to take care of us financially. The world doesn't work that way anymore." —*Joan Borysenko, medical doctor*

"People who have connected only to their families may be more vulnerable than those who connect more broadly. We need to learn how to be alone. You do that by developing depth within yourself, interests that are yours, a connection to something larger than yourself. You develop your own sense of the meaning of life." —*Rachel Naomi Remen, medical doctor*

"I wouldn't dream of crowing about the knot I've just tied, at thirty-eight, if it weren't for the purpose of telling a crucial truth to my still-single sisters. And for once, it's a truth they'll enjoy hearing. That truth is: It's Never Too Late to Be Picky About Men." —*Tish Durkin, journalist*

"Some women—and nearly every older man—scoff at the idea that when it comes to sex, youth beats experience. Well, it does." —*Lynn Snowden Picket, writer*

"There's an Iris Murdoch quote that I'm always paraphrasing: 'Love is the extremely difficult realization that something other than oneself is real. Love, and so art and morals, is the discovery of reality.' " —*Zadie Smith, novelist*

"My own view, for what it's worth, is that sexuality is lovely. There cannot be too much of it." —*Paul Goodman, writer*

"As much as I've loved my sexual adventures—the outside-the-box positions, the chemical and organic enhancements, the accessories, the diverse locations, private and public—what satisfies me most profoundly, both physically and emotionally, is being in my own bed, Steve on top of me, pushing the hair off my face, staring into my eyes, and telling me he loves me . . . Funny that I once thought vanilla was bland, boring. Now I know it's a classic that never loses its sweetness."
—*Valerie Frankel, author*

"The key to unlocking your sexual confidence is to check your self-perception. Beauty is in the eye of the beholder—and you have to see yourself as beautiful before you can expect anyone else to." —*Phil McGraw, psychologist*

"Here's the closest thing I know to a genuine love spell: 'I'll always love you, and I really don't care what you do.' This is not a promise to stay in a relationship with someone whose behavior is destructive. It's a simple statement that you aren't dependent on the other person's choices. That means you can respond to someone as he or she really is, instead of trying to force a fallible person to be infallible."
—*Martha Beck, life coach*

"You teach people how to treat you."

—*Phil McGraw, psychologist*

"Real love is a permanently self-enlarging experience."

—*M. Scott Peck, psychiatrist*

"Sex is hardly ever just about sex." —*Shirley MacLaine, actress*

"Intense physical passion waxes and wanes. Once you've had it, it can always come back. But what sustains you in between is having something that interests you both enough that you can share it, talk about it, do it together." —*Ethel Person, medical doctor and psychoanalyst*

"Real love is a verb. It's a behavior in which the welfare of another person is the primary intention and goal."

—*Harville Hendrix, author*

"I believe that the choice to become a mother is the choice to become one of the greatest spiritual teachers there is."

—*Oprah*

"Sex is a conversation carried out by other means."

—*Peter Ustinov, actor*

"Maybe your mother wasn't the kind of nurturing presence you longed for. You might have come from a home where your worth was seldom validated . . . But you make the choice: Will you languish in a history you can't revise or begin scripting a new experience? . . . You've been raised. Now rise above it."
—*Oprah*

"Here's what I learned: In order for dating to work, stop trying to make it work. I don't mean to suggest that you'll suddenly be having the time of your life. I found dating—my three-year bout of it—difficult and challenging and sometimes heartrending. But I was determined to approach it with a gentleness for myself and the other sorry sot across from me, and to breathe, breathe, breathe through it all. What a difference that has made."
—*Lise Funderburg, writer*

"Love . . . is transcending the ego to connect with another."
—*Joan Konner, journalist*

"For some reason, society does have the preconceived notion that in order to be a whole individual, we have to be half of a couple. Nothing could be further from the truth . . . If you have a life rich with friends, family, and career, you're blessed well beyond millions of people who are married and miserable."
—*Phil McGraw, psychologist*

"The pleasure of love is in loving."

—*François, duc de La Rochefoucauld, writer*

"Love doesn't just sit there like a stone; it has to be made, like bread, remade all the time, made new." —*Ursula K. Le Guin, writer*

"We are most alive when we are in love."

—*John Updike, author*

"For one human being to love another human being: That is perhaps the most difficult task that has been entrusted to us, the ultimate task." —*Rainer Maria Rilke, poet*

"Married or single, if you're looking for a sense of completion, I encourage you to look inward . . . The irony of relationships is that you're usually not ready for one until you can say from the deepest part of yourself, 'I will never again give up my power to another person.' Only then will you be a woman who's ready for the strongest kind of connection."
—*Oprah*

"The first duty of love is to listen." —*Paul Tillich, philosopher*

"This is what marriage really means: helping one another to reach the full status of being persons, responsible and autonomous beings who do not run away from life." —*Paul Tournier, physician and author*

"Intimacy is what makes a marriage, not a ceremony, not a piece of paper from the state." —*Kathleen Norris, poet*

"I used to believe that marriage would diminish me, reduce my options. That you had to be someone less to live with someone else when, of course, you have to be someone more." —*Candice Bergen, actress*

"A successful marriage requires falling in love many times, always with the same person." —*Mignon McLaughlin, journalist*

"If you feel a hunger for total nurturing—someone continuously anticipating your needs—don't start dating. Start therapy." —*Martha Beck, life coach*

"Passion is the quickest to develop, and the quickest to fade. Intimacy develops more slowly, and commitment more gradually still." —*Robert Sternberg, psychologist*

"Grown-up love is not sought at any cost or pursued with a sense of desperation. Yes, a relationship requires work. Yes, it means sacrifice. Yes, it's about compromise. But if it's healthy, it should bring you joy not just some of the time but most of the time. And whether you're twenty-five or forty-five, single or married, it should involve bringing all of who you are to the table—and walking away together with even more." —*Oprah*

"A successful marriage is an edifice that must be rebuilt every day." —*André Maurois, author*

"In courtship, you're trying to win the partner, keep the partner, stir up passion. With real love, the behaviors look the same but they arise out of the depth of the relationship and are expressed as a sense of gratitude. They come from within to reflect a state of being rather than to generate emotions." —*Harville Hendrix, author*

"The final word is love." —*Dorothy Day, journalist*

"One marries many times at many levels within a marriage. If you have more marriages than you have divorces within the marriage, you're lucky and you stick it out." —*Ruby Dee, actress*

"Anyone with a shattered heart can win the prize—a happier life, a happier relationship next time around—but only by making use of the mess right there in front of you. You have to think about it. Feel it. Mourn it. Miss him . . . And if you do all that, really breathe the sorrow, and let the sadness frame each beat of your heart, you'll not only be able to let it go, you'll find yourself arriving in a new place."
—*Lise Funderburg, writer*

"I'll take flannel sheets over silk any day of the week, rose petals make my eyes itchy, and I consider long baths incredibly tedious. I do, however, find sex—not the slick MTV kind, but the exuberant, klutzy, tender, funny, fiery, mystical, adventurous, creative kind—endlessly fascinating. I'm not sure what love's got to do with it, but I believe 'like' helps a lot and lust is essential." —*Lisa Kogan, writer*

"No one has the perfect love. It doesn't exist in the real world. Next time you measure yourself against an ideal, remember: June and Ward Cleaver had a set designer and a script."
—*Oprah*

"Fair or unfair, sometimes we have to give ourselves what we wish we could get from someone else."
—*Phil McGraw, psychologist*

"Life is not about a plan, because if you live by a plan, you're going to die by a plan . . . I never know at the beginning of a day what the end of the day will bring for us as a family, because we just go for it and do things." —*Kelly Ripa, television host*

"In the courtship, you catch up on everything you didn't know about each other's life up to that point. You keep unveiling secrets until there are none left to know. But then? What's left? Only this: the rest of your life . . . A change takes place, and it remains a secret to the two of you until the moment comes that you turn to your partner and say what's on your mind. And then the two of you know: This is who you are now, which is not who you were before, and which is not who you will be soon." —*Richard Panek, writer*

"People who are lousy with credit are lousy with relationships." —*Su̧e Orman, finance expert*

"Love cannot survive if you just give it scraps of yourself, scraps of your time, scraps of your thoughts." —*Mary O'Hara, singer*

"The definition of a friend is someone who's coming in the door when everybody else is going out." —*Phil McGraw, psychologist*

"Support the arts and improve your sex life. Get a sex book so you can talk to your partner about Practices That Cannot Be Mentioned. This includes those things that you would love to try or improve ("Hey, honey, that looks like fun"), and those less appealing that inspire 'Mother of God, please don't let that happen to me!' " —*Amy Bloom, author*

"Just last night I was laughing so hard on the phone with my friend Gayle that my head started to hurt. She was confronting me about a bad hair day and wanted to be sure I was aware that my 'do' wasn't doing it for me. Mid-howl, I thought, Isn't this a gift—after twenty-odd years of nightly phone calls, to have someone who tells me the truth and to laugh this loudly about it? I call that five-star pleasure." —*Oprah*

"Compartmentalize: If you must have a talk that you think could turn contentious, choose a window of time, address the issue, and move on." —*Phil McGraw, psychologist*

"Here are the real rules: Don't run with scissors, don't leave the iron on, don't cross against the light, and don't be afraid of a broken heart." —*Lise Funderburg, writer*

"My friends are my estate." —*Emily Dickinson, poet*

"Most men want the admiration of women—their smiles, their attention, their interest. That's why we beat our chests; that's why we play basketball and football. We want to know how you feel about us." —*Jamie Foxx, actor*

"Sex—when it's meaningful—can be a sublime expression of love. When it's not, well, it can be even better." —*Lisa Kogan, writer*

"There's no sanctuary more qualified to restore one's sense of humanity . . . than time spent around a dinner table with one's family and friends." —*Terrance Brennan, chef*

"Family, friends, food, and beautiful flourishes are life's graces, and we ought to celebrate them every day." —*Donata Maggipinto, author*

"The opposite of love is indifference." —*Phil McGraw, psychologist*

"I don't care if your best friend is dating a disgruntled postal employee with a shotgun collection: before you presume to advise her, check your judgments at the door." —*Martha Beck, life coach*

"For most women, friendship is a mutual advisory society; we tell one another our problems and hope to get a solution in return. However, the person asking for counsel is almost invariably the one best equipped to provide it." —*Martha Beck, life coach*

"When you're standing there taking your vows and wearing your beautiful white dress, few will tell you that you're entering into one of the most challenging agreements of your life. It's true that a great relationship can help you reach your highest potential. But it's also true that getting there is about much more than romance." —*Oprah*

"Sex and intimacy are not the same thing. You can have sex all your life and never be intimate with a person. There has to be empathy in the relationship. You have to enjoy seeing through their eyes. When you're with them, you're there and not thinking about what you're gonna do tomorrow." —*Jane Fonda, actress*

"If you have friends who base everything on their own and other people's appearances, ask yourself what you're getting out of the relationship. If it's mostly stress, it's time to find new friends." —*Laure Redmond, life coach*

"There are great parents of small children—they keep their little hair in bows—but those parents are not always good parents of young adults. As soon as their children get up to some size, it's 'Shut up, sit down, you talk too much, keep your distance, I'll send you to Europe!' My mom was a terrible parent of small children but a great parent of young adults. She'd talk to me as if I had some sense." —*Maya Angelou, author*

"It is the loving, not the loved woman who feels lovable." —*Jessamyn West, author*

"What happens in the first four minutes of togetherness sets the tone for the rest of your day or evening. So use that time to connect, acknowledge each other, and have fun." —*Phil McGraw, psychologist*

"Great sex is not a pleasant soak in the tub, with the scented candle burning. Great sex is more like a bomb exploding inside your right mind, leaving you with the shattered remains of your inhibitions, strange marks on the walls, and the telltale feeling: 'Kill me now, honey, it don't get no better than this.'" —*Amy Bloom, author*

"Accept what people offer. Drink their milkshakes. Take their love." —*Wally Lamb, author*

"Although aunting will never give me anything like the full course of motherhood, it does give me a wonderful, powerful—and possibly sufficient—taste of it. While I will never be the children's mother, I will always be their family, with all the history, complexity, and fidelity that entails. I couldn't drop them like a yoga class, a book club, or a waning friendship, even if I wanted to. I have known them forever, and they have known me." —*Tish Durkin, journalist*

"While pointing out a mistake, bring up the good things the other person has done. If you do that, then the person sees that you have a complete picture of him. There is nothing more dangerous than one who has been humiliated, even when you humiliated him rightly." —*Nelson Mandela, former president of South Africa*

"Do exactly what your 'Yeah-but' says you shouldn't. Write that novel. Adopt a puppy. Resist oppression. Keep the 'yeah' and kick the 'but.'" —*Martha Beck, life coach*

"So many people approach potential mates as if they were prizes and the point was winning, not knowing and being known." —*Amy Bloom, author*

"Passion—including the manifestations of passion we feel within ourselves and therefore call 'ours'—is not something we can grasp or own but a force of nature, connected to and influenced by things that extend far beyond any puny human self. Finding it isn't like bagging an expensive trinket; it's like leaving comfortable, familiar terrain behind us and throwing ourselves into the sea." —*Martha Beck, life coach*

"The key is to keep company only with people who uplift you, whose presence calls forth your best." —*Epictetus, philosopher*

"When people show you who they are, believe them."
—*Maya Angelou, author*

"I believe in love. I believe it transforms, transports, and transcends. I believe it fine-tunes goodness, solidifies strength, ripens resolve, eradicates rage, alleviates stress, and elevates empathy." —*Lisa Kogan, writer*

"My ability to get through my day greatly depends on the relationships that I have with other women . . . We have to be able to champion other women. We have to root for each other's successes and not delight in one another's failures." —*Michelle Obama, First Lady*

"People who don't feel good about themselves feel even worse when those around them do well. When they say, 'Who does she think she is?' what they really mean is 'How dare she exceed my expectations of who I think she should be?' . . . 'Who does she think she is?' also translates to 'Who do I think I'm not?'" —*Oprah*

"Most confident, successful men are inspired by ambitious women and actually seek them out. These enlightened men understand that their own interests are often advanced by the energy, drive, compassion, and style of a strong woman."
—*Mellody Hobson, finance manager and businesswoman*

"We believe that if we had a bigger house, more expensive clothes, or more academic degrees, people would value us more. But success is a currency that is not accepted by the heart: you can't buy love. Only people who are caught in the same misconception will bond with your accomplishment. Success-based relationships are parasitic, and they vanish when the fame, money, and power do." —*Martha Beck, life coach*

"With the gift of listening comes the gift of healing."
—*Catherine de Hueck Doherty, social activist*

"I wouldn't be who I am without my friends, many of whom I work with, create with, and bond with daily. I rely on them to tell me the truth. To keep me grounded. To keep this big life I live in perspective. My friends are my therapy, my release, my sounding board—my safe harbor." —*Oprah*

"If you cringe at the idea of looking at yourself in the mirror—with or without clothes—how can you possibly present yourself proudly to the world? I passionately believe that it's time to silence your harshest critic—you—and love your body in all its imperfect but unique glory." —*Laure Redmond, life coach*

"After conversing with everyone from homemakers and schoolteachers to corporate leaders and politicians, I know one thing for sure: Great communication begins with connection. What makes us different from one another is so much less important than what makes us alike—we all long for acceptance and significance." —*Oprah*

"Most of my friends are still amazed that my then-boyfriend (now husband) moved across the country with me a few years ago when I took a new job—despite the fact that women follow men for similar reasons all the time." —*Michelle Cottle, journalist*

"The moment you put a mental label on another human being, you can no longer truly relate to that person." —*Eckhart Tolle, spiritual teacher*

"Call it a clan, call it a network, call it a tribe, call it a family. Whatever you call it, whoever you are, you need one." —*Jane Howard, novelist*

"Sometimes being a friend means mastering the art of timing. There is a time for silence. A time to let go . . . And a time to prepare to pick up the pieces when it's all over." —*Gloria Naylor, author*

"Intimacy is not something that's achieved once and for all. It's lost and regained many times in the best of relationships. Knowing how to reestablish intimacy in the face of vulnerability, during those difficult times—that's the key to a loving, lasting relationship." —*Ellen Wachtel, writer*

"Friendship with oneself is all-important because without it one cannot be friends with anyone else in the world." —*Eleanor Roosevelt, former First Lady*

"A friend is a second self." —*Aristotle, philosopher*

"A lack of intimacy is not distance from someone else; it's disregard for yourself . . . If you're looking for someone to heal and complete you—to shush that voice inside you that has always whispered, You're not worth anything—you are wasting time. Why? Because if you don't already know that you have worth, there's nothing your friend, your family, or your mate can say that will completely assure you of that."
—*Oprah*

"People have two needs: one is to be intimate, the other is to be independent. The greatest barrier to intimacy is the fear that closeness will get in the way of independence. Intimacy is realizing that each person is the custodian of their partner's self-respect." —*Mildred Newman and Bernard Berkowitz, psychologists and married couple*

"She is a friend of my mind . . . The pieces I am, she gather them up and give them back to me in all the right order."
—*From* Beloved *by Toni Morrison, author and Nobel Prize recipient*

"There are people whom one loves immediately and forever. Even to know they are alive in the world with one is quite enough." —*Nancy Spain, journalist*

"The particular human chain we're part of is central to our individual identity." —*Elizabeth Stone, author*

"If someone tells me, 'Oh, I like your slacks,' and the man I'm with says, 'I don't. I wish she hadn't worn them,' I say, 'Oh, my dear—here are your keys.'" —*Maya Angelou, author*

"To be intimate is to be totally transparent, emotionally naked in front of another who is equally transparent. You want to see into the other person's heart. What people should mean when they say intimacy is in-to-me-see." —*Jeffrey L. Fine, psychologist*

"There's no single template for friendship. Some people are in our lives because they carry a precious shard of our history, while others reflect our passions and priorities right now." —*Barbara Graham, writer*

"Conflict in close relationships is not only inevitable, it's essential. Intimacy connects people who are inevitably different—as the saying goes, if two people agree about everything, one of them is superfluous. Conflict is the mechanism by which we set boundaries around these differences, so that each party feels safe with the other." —*Martha Beck, life coach*

"My friend is one . . . who takes me for what I am."
—*Henry David Thoreau, philosopher*

"Oh, the comfort—the inexpressible comfort of feeling safe with a person—having neither to weigh thoughts nor measure words, but pouring them all right out, just as they are, chaff and grain together, certain that a faithful hand will take and sift them, keep what is worth keeping, and then with the breath of kindness, blow the rest away."
—*Dinah Maria Mulock Craik, poet and novelist*

"Creating authentic intimacy with those you love means sometimes turning off the TV and phone, closing your mouth, opening your ears, and really paying attention."
—*Oprah*

"We all have our own closely guarded reality consisting of wants, needs, fears, prides, hopes, and dreams. No one can have intimate knowledge of you, and therefore an intimate relationship with you, unless you allow that person into your private world . . . There is no intimacy without vulnerability; there is no vulnerability without risk."
—*Phil McGraw, psychologist*

"You only live once—but if you work it right, once is enough."
—*Joe E. Lewis, comedian*

"It's the ones you can call up at four A.M. that matter."
—*Marlene Dietrich, actress and singer*

"The more shared past there is in a relationship, the more present you need to be; otherwise, you will be forced to relive the past again and again." —*Eckhart Tolle, spiritual teacher*

＊

"THE CHANCE TO LOVE AND BE LOVED EXISTS NO MATTER WHERE YOU ARE. MOST OF US CAN'T SEE IT BECAUSE WE HAVE OUR OWN PRECONCEIVED IDEAS ABOUT WHAT IT IS (IT'S SUPPOSED TO KNOCK YOU OFF YOUR FEET AND MAKE YOU SWOON) AND HOW IT SHOULD APPEAR (IN A TALL, SLIM, WITTY, CHARMING PACKAGE). SO IF LOVE DOESN'T SHOW UP WRAPPED IN OUR PERSONAL FANTASY, WE FAIL TO RECOGNIZE IT." —OPRAH

GIVING THANKS
AND GIVING BACK

*

WHEN YOU FOCUS ON THE GOODNESS IN

YOUR LIFE, YOU CREATE MORE OF IT.

—OPRAH

"The best cure for worry, depression, melancholy, brooding is to go deliberately forth and try to lift with one's sympathy the gloom of someone else." —*Arnold Bennett, author*

"I want my life to be about more than just fame or jewelry or parties. Hip-hop has the power to change the world. I am here to lead by example." —*Sean Combs, entertainment executive*

"The only gift is a portion of thyself."
—*Ralph Waldo Emerson, philosopher*

"I pray for all of us, oppressor and friend, that together we succeed in building a better world through human understanding and love." —*Fourteenth Dalai Lama, Buddhist leader*

"Over the years, I've heard people lament about why God allows this or that. Babies starve and people suffer not because of what God does, but because of what we don't do." —*Oprah*

"Never doubt that a small group of thoughtful, committed citizens can change the world. Indeed, it is the only thing that ever has." —*Margaret Mead, anthropologist*

"A year after I launched the book club, a woman who appeared on the show said something I'll never forget: 'Before I joined the book club, I had never read an entire book.' Reading has always been an open window to other worlds. Had I not been taught to read at an early age, I'd be an entirely different person. Thanks to books, I knew there was another kind of life. The chance to give another person that same gift? That was one of my proudest moments." —*Oprah*

"All I can do is be the best me that I can. And live life with some gusto. Giving back is a big part of that." —*Michelle Obama, First Lady*

"I see each day as another opportunity to get off my butt and make a difference in someone's life."
—*Holly Robinson Peete, actress*

"I believe in karma and doing the right thing even if it might not advance you as far as you want. If every single person felt the same way about karma, then the world would get fixed tomorrow." —*Shawn "Jay Z" Carter, entertainment executive*

"The habit of giving only enhances the desire to give."
—*Walt Whitman, poet*

"The world belongs to us, and it also belongs to us to change it. That's what I want people to know. [My husband] Danny got killed in the hands of people who are racist and intolerant, but Danny was the opposite. And they would want me to become intolerant and racist—but twice more now, I say the world belongs to me. That is Danny's legacy."
—*Mariane Pearl, widow of slain journalist Daniel Pearl*

"The first generosity may well be attentive respect."
—*Marilynne Robinson, novelist*

"We make a living by what we get. We make a life by what we give." —*Winston Churchill, British statesman*

"There is nothing in life more liberating than to fight for something more than yourself." —*John McCain, U.S. senator*

"In the end, giving [money] is about love. Your most important gift is not the check you write. Your most important gift is your openness to changing the life of the recipient, and to changing your own." —*Timothy Shriver, Special Olympics chairman*

"If you are not giving—and receiving—every day, you become a stagnant pool of pinch and grab and clutch, which is hell. A generous spirit is heaven. Rejoice in whatever occasional myopia you can muster. Most people are doing poorly, and you really can't help much. Feel sad. Pray. Give away more money. And then take a nap, or go buy lipstick. Breathe, eat well, pray, celebrate, too." —*Anne Lamott, writer*

"The best gift anyone can give, I believe, is the gift of sharing themselves . . . Every gift is your way of expressing how you feel about another person. I know for sure that's what we're here to do: keep the joy thing going for all seasons." —*Oprah*

"That's what I consider true generosity. You give your all, and yet you always feel as if it costs you nothing." —*Simone de Beauvoir, philosopher*

"Our great-grandmothers marched, were arrested, and suffered heroically in jail to obtain the vote for women. People walked the dusty back roads of the South, and sometimes died, to ensure African-Americans the right to vote. We should be humbled by that. We have progressed to where we are because we stand on all their shoulders, and we must never forget it. Voting says thank you." —*Ted Kennedy, former U.S. senator*

"It is well to give when asked, but it is better to give unasked, through understanding." —*Khalil Gibran, poet*

"I know for sure that when you shift your paradigm to what you can do for others, you begin to celebrate your own evolution and trigger a bounty of blessings." —*Oprah*

"There is only one real deprivation, I decided this morning, and that is not to be able to give one's gifts to those one loves most." —*May Sarton, poet*

"Anything that is of value in life only multiplies when it is given." —*Deepak Chopra, spiritual teacher*

"Giving is a necessity sometimes . . . more urgent, indeed, than having." —*Margaret Lee Runbeck, author*

"A gift—be it a present, a kind word, or a job done with care and love—explains itself! . . . And if receivin' it embarrasses you, it's because your 'thanks box' is warped." —*Alice Childress, actress*

"The fragrance always remains in the hand that gives the rose." —*Hada Bejar, actress*

"If my hands are fully occupied in holding on to something, I can neither give nor receive." —*Dorothee Sölle, theologian*

"Make a gratitude journal for someone you love, listing all the reasons you're grateful to have him or her in your life. This is the best gift ever!" —*Oprah*

"To have and not to give is often worse than to steal." —*Baroness Marie von Ebner-Eschenbach, writer*

"A gift, with a kind countenance, is a double present." —*Thomas Fuller, physician*

"The spirit in which a thing is given determines that in which the debt is acknowledged; it's the intention, not the face value of the gift, that's weighed." —*Seneca, philosopher*

"I happen to love giving. Even when I was a youngster and didn't have much to give, whatever I had or did was more enjoyable when I shared it. I used to love notebook paper, and I would bring five hundred sheets at a time to school. Whenever my classmates asked to borrow a sheet, I'd give them ten or twenty. It's the spirit of giving, not the largesse of the gift, that matters most." —*Oprah*

"Hospitality is supposedly something we do for others, but whenever I have guests (even those who don't buy me towels), I feel like I'm reaping the benefits. Hospitality involves sharing an intimate, private space—your home—and letting someone in shows trust. It shows that we're committed to lasting relationships with our friends, not just quick coffees when it's convenient." —*Lauren F. Winner, author*

"How we treasure (and admire) the people who acknowledge us! A simple gesture goes such a long way." —*Julie Morgenstern, organization expert*

"Everyone has the power for greatness, not for fame, but greatness, because greatness is determined by service." —*Martin Luther King Jr., civil rights leader and Nobel Peace Prize recipient*

"One single grateful thought raised to heaven is the most perfect prayer." —*G. E. Lessing, philosopher*

"You receive from the world what you give to the world. I understand it from physics as the third law of motion: for every action, there's an equal and opposite reaction. It is the essence of what Eastern philosophers call karma. In *The Color Purple*, the character Celie explained it to Mister: 'Everything you try to do to me, already done to you.'" —*Oprah*

"Gratitude is nice, but ingratitude is better. I want women to be angry at the injustices that remain, to have higher hopes. We get radicalized by seeing what could be better." —*Gloria Steinem, women's rights activist*

"Let us be grateful to the people who make us happy; they are the charming gardeners who make our souls blossom." —*Marcel Proust, novelist*

"The point is not to pay back kindness but to pass it on." —*Julia Alvarez, author*

"If the only prayer you ever say in your whole life is 'Thank you,' that would suffice." —*Meister Eckhart, theologian*

"Gratitude is the most exquisite form of courtesy."
—*Jacques Maritain, philosopher*

"It's not easy being grateful all the time. But it's when you feel least thankful that you are most in need of what gratitude can give you." —*Oprah*

"Every time we remember to say, 'Thank you,' we experience nothing less than heaven on earth." —*Sarah Ban Breathnach, author*

"Any act of appreciation affirms our connection to each other. Validates us. Expands who we are in the world. Deepens our spirit. And can turn an ordinary moment into an extraordinary, peachy, and praiseful day." —*Oprah*

"This is the true joy in life, the being used for a purpose recognized by yourself as a mighty one . . . the being a force of Nature instead of a feverish selfish little clod of ailments and grievances complaining that the world will not devote itself to making you happy." —*George Bernard Shaw, playwright*

"Just to be is a blessing; just to live is holy."
—*Rabbi Abraham Heschel, theologian*

"Abundance is, in large part, an attitude."
—*Sue Patton Thoele, author*

"Silent gratitude isn't much use to anyone."
—*Gladys Bronwyn Stern, author*

"Whenever you can't think of something to be grateful for, remember your breath. With each breath you take, you can say, 'I am still here.'" —*Oprah*

"We must be the change we wish to see in the world."
—*Mahatma Gandhi, former political and spiritual leader of India*

"Each moment in time we have it all, even when we think we don't." —*Melody Beattie, counselor*

"Feeling grateful to or appreciative of someone or something actually attracts more of the things that you appreciate and value in your life." —*Christiane Northrup, medical doctor and women's wellness expert*

"For all that has been, thanks. For all that will be, yes."
—*Dag Hammarskjöld, diplomat*

"For today and its blessings, I owe the world an attitude of gratitude." —*Clarence E. Hodges, former U.S. commissioner for the Administration of Children, Youth, and Families*

"The next time you find yourself surrounded by darkness in the middle of a storm and everything is at its absolute worst, take a moment to give thanks—because you know that no matter what, the sun is going to rise. It will get better. That is sunrise faith." —*Oprah*

"Happiness is when what you think, what you say, and what you do are in harmony." —*Mahatma Gandhi, former political and spiritual leader of India*

"Most folks are about as happy as they make up their minds to be." —*Abraham Lincoln, sixteenth president of the United States*

"I have come to believe that giving and receiving are really the same. Giving and *receiving*—not giving and taking." —*Joyce Grenfell, actress and comedian*

"We can't take any credit for our talents. It's how we use them that counts." —*Madeleine L'Engle, author*

" 'When you learn, teach. When you get, give.' That's another one of my favorite quotes from Maya Angelou. What I know for sure is that what you give comes back to you. That's not just my theory or point of view—it's physics. Life is an energy exchange of giving and receiving, and the way to have what you want is to give what you need."
—Oprah

"No one is useless in this world who lightens the burdens of another." *—Charles Dickens, novelist*

"The truth is the kindest thing we can give folks in the end."
—Harriet Beecher Stowe, American abolitionist and author

"Before you go to bed tonight, make a blessings list. If you don't go to sleep with a sense of joy in your heart, one of us is a fool." *—Phil McGraw, psychologist*

"There is nothing more visceral than cynicism, nothing more brutish than greed. These are reflexes, common and unremarkable, of the undeveloped spirit. But charity in its finest sense is always an act of the creative imagination." *—Charles P. Pierce, sportswriter*

"If you knew what I know about the power of giving, you would not let a single meal pass without sharing it in some way." —*Buddha, spiritual teacher*

"As I seek the comfort to give, I know that what I've found in the search is comfort for myself, the consolation that comes from accompanying a friend on her journey as far as I can go, however steep the way." —*Catherine Calvert, writer*

✳

"I LIVE IN THE SPACE OF THANKFULNESS—AND I HAVE BEEN REWARDED A MILLION TIMES OVER FOR IT. I STARTED OUT GIVING THANKS FOR THE SMALL THINGS, AND THE MORE THANKFUL I BECAME, THE MORE MY BOUNTY INCREASED. THAT'S BECAUSE WHAT YOU FOCUS ON EXPANDS, AND WHEN YOU FOCUS ON THE GOODNESS IN YOUR LIFE, YOU CREATE MORE OF IT."
—OPRAH

JOY, FUN,
AND PLEASURE

*

I DEFINE JOY AS A SUSTAINED SENSE
OF WELL-BEING AND PEACE—A CONNECTION
TO WHAT MATTERS.

—OPRAH

"Surely joy is the condition of life."
—*Henry David Thoreau, philosopher*

"One of the secrets of a happy life is continuous small treats."
—*Iris Murdoch, novelist*

"To love what you do and feel that it matters—how can anything be more fun?" —*Katherine Graham, publisher*

"There may be times in a girl's life when it's better to be boyless, but there's no need to be joyless. Or toyless."
—*Cindy Chupack, author*

"I know for sure that I don't want to live a shut-down life—desensitized to feeling, seeing, and the possibility of experiencing joy on every level. I want every day to be a fresh start on expanding what is possible. And I also know that one person can make a huge difference." —*Oprah*

"You're worried about how you're going to feel at the end of your life? What about right now? Live. Right this minute. That's where the joy's at." —*Abigail Thomas, writer*

"In my music, I try to be as truthful as I can. I'm not sure I can be as honest in my life as I can be in my music, because with manners comes insincerity. Like 'How are you?' 'I'm very well.' But I'm not. I have a massive hangover . . . Joy is the hardest possible thing to contrive as an act."
—*Bono, rock musician*

"In life there will be sickness, devastation, heartache—it's a given . . . If you look hard enough, you can always find the bright side." —*Rashida Jones, actress*

"Play is one of those things—like dreaming—that seems superfluous but we cannot live without . . . Good play, by nature, is therapeutic . . . While trauma and threat tend to take away the desire for playfulness, they intensify the need for it. To live through uncertain times, we cannot exist solely in a state of apprehension." —*Mark Epstein, psychiatrist*

"To be quite oneself one must first waste a little time." —*Elizabeth Bowen, author*

"My former boss, the general manager, said to me, 'There's no way you can make it in Chicago up against Donahue' . . . He used every tactic he could muster to entice me to stay—more money, a company car, a new apartment, and finally, intimidation: 'You're going to fail.' . . . I gathered the nerve to say to him before standing up to walk out, 'You're right, I may not make it, and I may be walking into unforeseen land mines. But if they don't kill me, at least I'll keep growing. I've grown all I can here. I have to move on.' In that moment, I chose happiness." —*Oprah*

"My happiness is not the means to any end. It is the end." —*Ayn Rand, author*

"I'm always happy with whatever I have. If I can get something else, great. If I lose half of everything tomorrow, fine. That's why I don't buy anything on credit. If everything is over with now, I still have what I have. If everything ended tomorrow, I'd say, 'Well, I did okay. That was a good run.'"
—*Jay Leno, television host*

"Getting what you go after is success; but liking it while you are getting it is happiness." —*Bertha Damon, writer*

"It's not that I'm sweet as pie every day at work. But I take work as a joyous responsibility." —*Julia Roberts, actress*

"Money often compounds unhappiness because, mistakenly, we think that spending will make us feel better . . . When you're happy, you create your own financial stability by living within your means." —*Suze Orman, finance expert*

"How do you find what's going to make everybody have this strange reaction in their bodies, this response that's sort of chemical and physical at once—this noise and emotion that changes how you sit? A laugh is a weird sound . . . But when I can feel proud of myself for causing it, it's really great."
—*Billy Crystal, comedian*

"Happiness is neither virtue nor pleasure, nor this thing nor that, but simply growth." —*W. B. Yeats, poet*

"The moments of happiness we enjoy take us by surprise. It is not that we seize them, but that they seize us." —*Ashley Montagu, anthropologist*

"Mix a little foolishness with your prudence: it's good to be silly at the right moment." —*Horace, satirist*

"Life is to be enjoyed, not simply endured. Pleasure and goodness and joy support the pursuit of survival." —*Willard Gaylin, ethicist*

"You may feel stuck—trapped in a bad relationship, grieving over a divorce, miserably and interminably single—but it is in your power, and your best health interest, to choose joy. Okay, so you can't find romance. Or your soul mate doesn't feel the same way about you. But you can put yourself in the path of happiness. You can fall in love with life." —*Lesley Dorman, journalist*

"The worst sin—perhaps the only sin—passion can commit, is to be joyless." —*Dorothy L. Sayers, writer*

"I take my pleasure seriously. I work hard and pleasure well; I believe in the yin and yang of life. It doesn't take a lot to make me happy because I take pleasure from everything I do."
—*Oprah*

"To understand the true nature of pleasure, borrow an amiable infant. Dip your finger in sugar, offer it to the baby, and watch her intently gum the treat. As the sensation of sweetness fires various brain synapses, the baby's facial muscles will relax. Her tongue will protrude, flick in and out. A dreamy smile may light up her face. This is one happy baby."
—*Gretchen Reynolds, author*

"Sometimes I laugh out loud just remembering someone else laughing out loud. Why does it feel so good to make someone laugh? Because it's a selfish and generous action, both at the same time . . . When we make others laugh, it's exhilarating. It means someone was actually listening to us. Laughter also releases endorphins that ease pain, heartache, or sadness (or so the story goes). What a gift." —*Bonnie Hunt, actress*

"Music enters our bodies, commandeering the pulse in our veins, and reminds us that pleasure isn't a matter of feeling good but of feeling more alive." —*Holly Brubach, journalist*

"What I know for sure is that pleasure is energy reciprocated. What you put out comes back. Your base level of pleasure is determined by how you view your whole life."
—*Oprah*

"Most of us are brought up to think the key to happiness lies outside ourselves. We look to falling in love, having a family, making a career, or building a dream house, and we expect that these levels of accomplishment will be enough. But often we find that when one level of need is satisfied, another takes its place." —*Mark Epstein, psychiatrist*

"If we're stuck with having expectations, there's a very good reason to embrace positive ones: it's that we often create what we anticipate." —*Martha Beck, life coach*

"It is possible to live happily ever after on a day-to-day basis."
—*Margaret Wander Bonanno, writer*

"One can get just as much exultation in losing oneself in a little thing as in a big thing. It is nice to think how one can be so recklessly lost in a daisy!" —*Anne Morrow Lindbergh, aviation pioneer and author*

"To awaken quite alone in a strange town is one of the most pleasant sensations in the world. You are surrounded by adventure." —*Freya Stark, travel writer*

"When you die, God and the angels will hold you accountable for all the pleasure you were allowed in life that you denied yourself." —*Anonymous*

"As we watch someone else partake of the stockpile of joy, our hearts may sink—we're not going to get our share. But someone else's pleasure doesn't cause our unhappiness—we make ourselves unhappy because our negativity isolates us. An alternative to feeling painfully cut off is to learn to rejoice in the happiness of others." —*Sharon Salzberg, meditation teacher*

"Grief can take care of itself, but to get the full value of a joy, you must have somebody to divide it with." —*Mark Twain, novelist*

"Weeping may endure for a night, but joy cometh in the morning." —*Psalms 30:5*

"Joy is prayer. Joy is strength. Joy is love. Joy is a net of love by which you can catch souls." —*Mother Teresa, Catholic nun and Nobel Peace Prize recipient*

"True happiness . . . arises in the first place, from the enjoyment of one's self." —*Joseph Addison, essayist and poet*

"Learning to live in the present moment is part of the path of joy." —*Sarah Ban Breathnach, author*

"Winning is important to me, but what brings me joy is the experience of being fully engaged in whatever I'm doing." —*Phil Jackson, basketball coach*

"No self-help book, e-retailer, or bossy sister can tell you what will give you pleasure. To find it, you have to divine yourself, listen for a particular note, or be alert to a gentle itch of interest, then follow it through the maw and negative voices. And when you've gotten there, what you've found probably speaks profoundly to who you really are. That person is worth getting to know." —*Cynthia King, editor*

"Happiness depends on ourselves." —*Aristotle, philosopher*

"People believe themselves to be dependent on what happens for their happiness. They don't realize that what happens is the most unstable thing in the universe." —*Eckhart Tolle, spiritual teacher*

"Happiness comes of the capacity to feel deeply, to enjoy simply, to think freely, to risk life, to be needed."
—*Storm Jameson, writer*

"Real joy comes not from ease or riches or from the praise of men, but from doing something worthwhile."
—*Sir Wilfred Grenfell, missionary*

"Birds sing after a storm; why shouldn't people feel as free to delight in whatever sunlight remains to them?"
—*Rose Kennedy, philanthropist*

"Follow your bliss." —*Joseph Campbell, mythologist*

"Joy is not in things; it is in us." —*Richard Wagner, composer*

"When we blame our lack of joy on a lack of money, we are confusing who we are with what we have . . . True wealth is not measured by bank account balances alone but by the richness of your life on every level." —*Suze Orman, finance expert*

"All I can say about life is, Oh God, enjoy it!"
—*Bob Newhart, comedian*

"There is no such thing as a 'finished' person; whatever your circumstances are, it is your challenge to keep asking yourself the tough question that will move you forward in your life. What I've discovered is that joy isn't waiting on the other side of that process; joy *is* that process . . . The greatest joy lies not in simply being but in becoming."
—*Oprah*

"Joy and hope are never separate. I have never met a hopeful person who was depressed or a joyful person who had lost hope . . . It is important to become aware that at every moment of our life we have the opportunity to choose joy. It is in the choice that our true freedom lies, and that freedom is, in the final analysis, the freedom to love."
—*Henri J. M. Nouwen, pastor*

"I do not always practice what I preach and sit down to eat with all my family, but rather feed them and then sneak upstairs to eat my supper in bed. I compound this sin, but also my pleasure somehow, by not having a tray. I love beautiful linens and adore my bed, but I am uncaring about the spillage and drips and crumbs I leave in my lazy, greedy wake."
—*Nigella Lawson, food writer*

"During truffle season, I have pasta or risotto with white truffles, cream, and butter—multiple occasions a month. It's hallelujah time. I plan ahead, and I'm fanatical about it."
—*Colin Cowie, party planner*

"Every day brings a chance for you to draw in a breath, kick off your shoes, and step out and dance—to live free of regret and filled with as much joy, fun, and laughter as you can stand. You can either waltz boldly onto the floor of life and live the way you know your spirit is nudging you to, or you can sit quietly by the wall, receding in the shadows of fear and self-doubt. You have the choice this very moment—the only moment you have for certain." —*Oprah*

"Happiness is ever elusive, but freedom from unhappiness is attainable now, by facing what is rather than making up stories about it." —*Eckhart Tolle, spiritual teacher*

"Why learn a piece of music unless it's to be performed? Why knit a sweater unless it's to be given to a loved one? We think everything we do has to be up to snuff and we forget that the pure, uncensored joy of living in our skin comes when we are not attached, 24-7, to either our fans or our critics. We can paint just for ourselves. We can belt out torch songs in an empty office." —*Veronica Chambers, author and journalist*

"Humor can turn the serious into the bearable, the humiliating into the humbling, the mundane into the unique."
—*Lian Dolan, writer*

❋

"I DEFINE JOY AS A SUSTAINED SENSE OF WELL-BEING AND PEACE—A CONNECTION TO WHAT MATTERS . . . WHAT I KNOW FOR SURE IS THAT YOU FEEL REAL JOY IN DIRECT PROPORTION TO HOW CONNECTED YOU ARE TO LIVING YOUR TRUTH." —OPRAH

HONORING YOUR BODY, TRUSTING YOUR GUT

*

THIS IS THE BODY YOU'VE BEEN
GIVEN—LOVE WHAT YOU'VE GOT.
—OPRAH

"Real beauty isn't about symmetry or weight or makeup; it's about looking life right in the face and seeing all its magnificence reflected in your own." —*Valerie Monroe, writer*

"The more you release your defensive, self-conscious inner critic, the more you'll get smiles, courtesy, friendliness, all kinds of positive attention—not from everyone, but from most people. From enough people." —*Martha Beck, life coach*

"The body you're born with sculpts your personality as intricately and definingly as any life experience. For nearly eighteen years, my six-feet-seven-inches-ness made me shy, elusive, and vigilantly self-conscious . . . Twenty-five years later, I love being tall. What could be cooler? It's my pleasure to grab soup or cashews on high shelves for mothers in supermarkets. I like the fact that my kids won't ever lose me in a crowd."
—*Peter Smith, writer*

"I look at my very imperfect body and see its patches of history, like stamps on my passport. The stamps aren't the kind of thing that would make me throw off my towel at the gym or be the first to jump naked into a lake. But like a good story, they remind me of where I've been, and the annoying and endearing people I've met along the way."
—*Betsy Carter, writer*

"From certain angles, I liked my nose—still do. Some people would tell me, 'You could take the bump off.' And I would say, 'But I like the bump.'" —*Barbra Streisand, singer*

"Everybody has a part of her body that she doesn't like, but I've stopped complaining about mine because I don't want to critique nature's handiwork . . . My job is simply to allow the light to shine out of the masterpiece." —*Alfre Woodard, actress*

"I'd never actually paid attention to my hair; I'd only tried to flatten it out and hide it so people wouldn't peg me as different. It took a while, but as my hair grew, I began to appreciate how many textures exist on my scalp . . . Now I actually look forward to strangers asking, 'What do you use to get your hair like this?' It's called Multicontinent DNA. Cool, right?"
—*Angela Nissel, author and television producer*

"I can't say that overnight I stopped wanting to resemble someone else (or that I never do now), but I understand on a visceral level how deeply subjective beauty is, how wholly dependent on context, how mutable, how wide." —*Elizabeth Bern, writer*

"Whenever your gut is out of kilter, trouble awaits. Your gut is your inner compass. Whenever you have to consult other people for an answer, you're headed in the wrong direction."
—*Oprah*

"The best we can do is focus on what we have the power to improve in ourselves, and when it comes to body—love the one you're with." —*Sara Davidson, writer*

"Don't get hung up on the size. If you feel bad about yourself because a 12 is what fits, take a Sharpie, and write '6' on the label." —*Stacy London, fashion consultant*

"The irony of being a performer is that I have huge insecurities. People are shocked to hear that I think my legs are fat or I don't like the way I look. We all have insecurities. We'd be lying if we said we didn't . . . My job is to conquer my fears." —*Madonna, singer*

"Sometimes I climb from my marriage bed to the bathroom, and that long-loved look on my face—flushed and rumpled with pleasure—holds more beauty, I see clearly, than any of the plummy tautness of my younger self." —*Catherine Newman, author*

"I know the human body from the cradle to the grave. I'm a mother. I was an art student. I love bodies in every guise. They're nature, so by nature they're beautiful." —*Patricia Volk, author*

"I may wish I had different calves and thighs, and no knock-knees. But I like who I am as a person. And because I believe that there's much more to me than my looks, other people believe it, too." —*Felicia P. Fields, actress*

"If we looked at eating as an activity to relish rather than as an invitation to gluttony, we'd all be not only healthier but happier." —*Michelle Stacey, writer*

"Body hatred has been defined as a personal problem. But it is a social problem, a political problem, a cultural problem. It is not accidental or incidental. It is induced, injected, and programmed . . . The antidote to body hatred is social activism and community. None of us is strong enough to stand up to the daily onslaught of propaganda, imagery, programming, seduction, and mind control. But as a group, we can shift the tyranny." —*Eve Ensler, playwright*

"When we're awake in our bodies and senses, the world comes alive. Wisdom, creativity, and love are discovered as we relax and awaken through our bodies." —*Tara Brach, psychologist*

"Doubt means don't. Don't move. Don't answer. Don't rush forward." —*Oprah*

"Confidence is the sexiest thing a woman can have. It's much sexier than any body part." —*Aimee Mullins, model and amputee*

"To have that sense of one's intrinsic worth . . . is potentially to have everything." —*Joan Didion, journalist and author*

"Each individual woman's body demands to be accepted on its own terms." —*Gloria Steinem, women's rights activist*

"The moment I slipped into the wispy chiffon, my perception changed. When I looked in the mirror, I cried. I'm not kidding. I didn't know I could look like that. What I thought were bulges became curves, and what I was convinced was fat became pleasingly soft and round. There was someone beautiful looking back from the mirror, and after nearly forty years of life, I could see her." —*Amy Hertz, editor*

"Your life is speaking to you every day, all the time—and your job is to listen up and find the clues. Passion whispers to you through your feelings, beckoning you toward your highest good. Pay attention to what makes you feel energized, connected, stimulated—what gives you your juice." —*Oprah*

"Once, when I was about fifteen, my gym teacher had provoked a horrible crisis of self-image when she remarked, 'Your whole body changed this summer—look at you, you have childbearing hips!' I was appalled and hurt beyond any sane sense of what she had said. Now here it was finally, self-acceptance: freckles, fluffy hair, roundness, a slight flush to the cheeks. All good, and all me." —*Elaina Richardson, writer*

"Trust your instincts. Intuition doesn't lie." —*Oprah*

"I no longer look at every reflection of myself and see a map of disappointments. I see vigor, curves, and force, an organic tumble of sensual, sexual energy. I stand straighter. I breathe deeper. My heart opens." —*Lise Funderburg, writer*

"People always say, 'I'm too busy to exercise,' 'I have to be there for the kids,' 'I've got too much work.' You know what? These are little lies you're telling yourself, and they go against the laws of self-preservation, because the more whole and healthy you are, the more fully you can give to other people." —*Oprah*

"Say we're thinking about how to get skinnier. When we do that, we're on our way to somewhere else; we're not experiencing life right here. In the moments when we're trying to make things different, we're not spontaneous, we're not accessing our creativity or intuition, and most important—because living in our minds keeps us separate from each other—we can't really feel love." —*Tara Brach, psychologist*

"One of the most important laws of money is to trust yourself more than you trust anyone else . . . Your gut is telling you something." —*Suze Orman, finance expert*

"Consciously observe the stream of thoughts you direct toward your body (I need Botox. Why am I so dense? I hate, hate, hate my nose). Once you've noticed your own abusive mantras, begin countering each one with some sort of genuine praise . . . If you loathe your upper-arm flab, make yourself think about the fact that your arm, flab and all, can participate in procedures as delicate as threading a needle or as powerful as shifting a car in gear . . . This may feel absurd at first, but if you pay attention, you'll find that countering abuse with praise has a wonderful effect on your own body." —*Martha Beck, life coach*

"I gave the reflection in the mirror a last cheerful examination, adjusted the ridiculous hat slightly, and went out to rejoin the wedding—sure then as now that anyone who thinks that physical appearance alone is the key to success and happiness is both wrong and mad." —*Maeve Binchy, author*

"It is confidence in our bodies, minds, and spirits that allows us to keep looking for new adventures, new directions to grow in, and new lessons to learn—which is what life is all about." —*Oprah*

"Our bodies are our gardens, to the which our wills are gardeners." —*Othello* (Act I, Scene iii), *William Shakespeare, playwright*

"When I feel lost and can't make a decision, I just stop and get quiet. I take a time-out. I ask myself, How does this feel? What do I want my life to be like? I try not to listen to the shoulds or coulds, and try to get beyond expectations, peer pressure, or trying to please—and just listen. I believe all the answers are ultimately within us." —*Kim Cattrall, actress*

"Perhaps we don't want to believe that our staying too busy might be a cushion that protects us from the two things that scare us: silence and ourselves. But what would happen if we stopped and became a little less fearful of what we're feeling?" —*Arlie Russell Hochschild, author and sociologist*

"What if—lucky you—your parents were your devoted admirers, your mother liked her body, and your lover loves yours? Well, then, all you've got to deal with is the rigid and distorted American ideal of the beautiful female. Research indicates that she is 11 percent below normal weight. Fifteen percent below normal weight is considered anorexia." —*Valerie Monroe, writer*

"When you don't know what to do, my best advice is to do nothing until clarity comes." —*Oprah*

"I believe we discover our destinies in the smallest ways—in a fascination with words, in the thrill a child's laughter evokes, and even in a familiar song we keep humming. If you pay attention to these cues—to the times you've felt most joyous, most fully engaged, most connected with yourself and others—you'll always be guided to the next best place." —*Oprah*

"Most people don't realize how much time we spend imprisoned by a sense of falling short. And yet at any moment that we're judging ourselves insufficient, we can't relax and appreciate the life that's right here." —*Tara Brach, psychologist*

"In twenty years of working with patients, I've found that people will commit to change only when their motivation outweighs the challenges . . . Even if you're strongly motivated, though, doughnuts are tough to walk away from." —*David L. Katz, medical doctor and nutrition specialist*

"Now any woman can play adult dress-up and have fun as her breasts rise to the occasion. Why not? You're too old? Too flat? If you're thinking that cleavage is not for the mature, I say, So what if your treasure chest has become a bit weighty or tarnished by time? Those are meager reasons to quit enjoying your bounty." —*Valerie Monroe, writer*

"When I'm acting with new people, I try to tune in to what's going on. Are they distracted by something? Are they competitive? . . . Intuition is working all the time—you just have to listen to it." —*Pam Grier, actress*

＊

"I DID A HEAD-TO-TOE ASSESSMENT, AND THOUGH THERE WAS PLENTY OF ROOM FOR IMPROVEMENT, I NO LONGER HATED ANY PART OF MYSELF, INCLUDING THE CELLULITE. I THOUGHT, THIS IS THE BODY YOU'VE BEEN GIVEN—LOVE WHAT YOU'VE GOT. THIS IS THE FACE I WAS BORN WITH—THE SAME LINES I HAD UNDER MY EYES AT AGE TWO HAVE GOTTEN DEEPER, BUT THEY'RE MY LINES. THE SAME BROAD NOSE I TRIED TO HEIGHTEN WHEN I WAS EIGHT, BY SLEEPING WITH A CLOTHESPIN AND TWO COTTON BALLS ON THE SIDE, IS THE NOSE I'VE GROWN INTO. THE FULL LIPS I USED TO PULL IN WHEN SMILING ARE NOW THE LIPS I USE TO SPEAK TO MILLIONS OF PEOPLE EVERY DAY—MY LIPS NEED TO BE FULL."
—OPRAH

AHA MOMENTS

ONCE THE LIGHT BULB CAME ON FOR ME,
MY CALLING BECAME TO CREATE SHOWS THAT
ENCOURAGE AND INSPIRE AS MUCH AS
THEY ENTERTAIN.

—OPRAH

"Breakthroughs occur when you suddenly see something on the other side of the clutter that you desperately, vividly want. So let me give you an assignment. Ask yourself what is on the other side of *your* clutter? Are you ready to embrace it? Because the skills it takes to get organized are simple. Beyond that clutter, I promise you'll find the space and the time to fulfill your dreams." —*Julie Morgenstern, organization expert*

"Aha! I got it. Working out slows the aging process and makes you more vital. Aha! Aha! Aha!" —*Oprah*

"I've spent a lot of my life trying to make people comfortable, even though I'm not exactly sure why they aren't . . . I don't work anymore at trying to make sure others like me. I've given up on that. This is who I am." —*Maria Shriver, First Lady of California*

"The older I get, the more I think you must be kind. That's why I'll probably be less and less of a good interviewer. Sometimes you have to ask the tough questions. I can't be quite as brash as I used to be. I know it hurts. I've become a kinder person." —*Barbara Walters, television journalist*

"I used to be intimidated by celebrities. I remember early in my career, when I was about twenty-four . . . I had five minutes, tops, to establish a connection with the then unknown [actor] Robin Williams. Robin, who may have been wilder than he is today, was all over the place . . . I didn't know what to do, but knew instinctively that a normal conversation was not going to happen . . . So I took a deep breath and allowed myself to be carried by the flow of his excited energy . . . It's a lesson I never forgot: Find the flow and follow it." —*Oprah*

"I used to struggle to put a monetary value on my work . . . When I started my own firm, I found it so tough to bill for my services that I asked people to pay me what *they* thought my work was worth. To my amazement, people paid me more than I would ever have dreamed of billing them. It was an eye-opener. If others valued me more than I valued myself, I knew I needed a serious attitude adjustment."

—*Suze Orman, finance expert*

"I remind myself, while feeling afraid, to love life anyway, to retain the certain knowledge that I will die someday and use that to open to the preciousness of what I see and feel right in front of me. Now I might feel afraid but am determined to have that fear serve as a counterpoint to my tendency to procrastinate—if I have to apologize, tell someone 'I love you,' try to make a difference, I need to do it without delay."

—*Sharon Salzberg, meditation teacher*

"My intention to please was creating a logical effect. Others were so pleased that they'd often come back and ask me to do more! So I decided to become aware of my every intention in order to create a different outcome. That meant doing only those things that came from the truth of who I am—and only doing that which pleased me to do for others."

—*Oprah*

"After I had [my daughter] Malia, I began to prioritize exercise because I realized that my happiness is tied to how I feel about myself. I want my girls to see a mother who takes care of herself, even if that means I have to get up at four thirty so I can do a workout." —*Michelle Obama, First Lady*

"We're liberated from being better. I'm not going to have a better day, a more magical moment, than the first time I heard my daughter giggle. Tomorrow's not going to be better than that. So why invest in better? If God spoke to me right now and told me that I would never have greater stimuli than I have right now, that wouldn't worry me. It's all about how you celebrate the stimuli you have." —*Sean Penn, actor*

"First, I had to figure out how to ask [my future wife] out on a date. Actually, first I had to ask someone what her name was—Melania, a beautiful name—because I wasn't sure how to approach her myself. Considering my reputation for being anything but shy, my reaction might sound hard to believe, but it was a real aha moment for me: I realized that even after you've done a lot of living, you can still be amazed by what can turn up in life—that it's possible to discover things you hadn't thought existed." —*Donald Trump, entrepreneur*

"My big light bulb moment on relationships came the first time I talked with marriage therapist Harville Hendrix. He introduced me to the imago theory—in essence, he says it's not a coincidence that you've attracted your partner; that person is there to help you do the work of recovering from old wounds. That show changed me. I saw relationships not solely as the kind of romantic pursuit our society celebrates but as a spiritual partnership that's meant to change how you see yourself and the world." —*Oprah*

"I try very hard to go easy on the firm conclusions. These days I settle for feeling only 85 percent sure about most things, most of the time. I believe that is keeping me sane, and I also believe that it's keeping me human. In fact, I'm 85 percent sure of it."
—*Elizabeth Gilbert, writer*

"Most of the time when I look back on what I've done, I think, 'Did I do that?' And you know what I say to myself? Why didn't I enjoy it more? Was I working too hard to see it? . . . What I'm trying to do now, before it's too late, is to finally smell the roses. I know it's a cliché, but I want to enjoy it. I want to get rid of the alarm clock every day. I've done enough. Time is what it's all about." —*Barbara Walters, television journalist*

"I made a conscious decision not to move into my house and close the gate as I have for so many years . . . My life has a new, unexpected layer. I thought I was through making friends. But much to my surprise, I've found myself looking forward to hanging out, laughing, talking serious, and just connecting and embracing one another as part of the circle. It's added new meaning, a feeling of community I didn't even know I was missing." —*Oprah*

"I don't have to be perfect. All I have to do is show up and enjoy the messy, imperfect, and beautiful journey of my life. It's a trip more wonderful than I could have imagined."
—*Kerry Washington, actress*

"The first chance I got to wear one of [the designer] Valentino's gowns—meaning my pocketbook and my body were ready—was in 1994. I'd never felt more beautiful. I loved the dress and me in the dress so much that I told my friend Gayle, 'If I die in the near future, please have me buried in this.' . . . Valentino says your clothes should make you feel alive. They have to live with you and move with you. That's the key to elegance: not just wearing beautiful things, but making what you're wearing come alive." —*Oprah*

"If I didn't know better, I'd say I was thin. I do, however, know better—the fact is, I'm not thin. But here's my new-found reality: you don't have to be thin to look great."
—*Lisa Kogan, writer*

"When [my children] left home, I fell into a huge, empty, black hole. Your children are grown and your career has slowed down—all the stuff that took up so much attention is gone, and you're left with expansive time and space. You have to reimagine who are you and what life is all about. Photography was a blessing because it filled my time. If I had to start over, I'd pursue photography—probably to the exclusion of acting."
—*Jessica Lange, actress*

"When I was at Northwestern Memorial Hospital in Chicago, I began taking improv classes at a theater called Second City . . . I kept my job at the hospital and did shows at night. One night a patient named Rudy told me, 'You should go out to California and audition for stuff.' I said, 'Oh, I'd never do that. I'd be humiliated. I'd fail.' Rudy said, 'I'm at the end of my life. I only have a few weeks to live, and my biggest regret is that I feared failure. Promise me that when I'm gone, you'll go and fail many times in California.' We shook hands on it."
—*Bonnie Hunt, actress*

"I used to think that when you grew up, you actually stopped growing. How wrong I was." —*Katie Couric, television journalist*

"I've been so focused on getting to the next level, I haven't enjoyed the view from where I am. Years are a blur to me . . . because when you live a life in the fast lane, as I have, you end up speeding through, just moving to the next thing, doing more and more, and filling your schedule until there's no time even to think about what you're doing . . . With all that I know for sure, today I added this: It makes no difference how many peaks you reach if there was no pleasure in the climb." —*Oprah*

"We once went to a benefit where a band we wanted to hear was playing . . . I was shaking badly and people were coming up to me, hugging me and looking at me with that look I recognize. They're looking for fear in me. When they don't see that, they then see their own fear reflected back at them and they start to freak out . . . People look at me and think, My God, could that happen to me? And when I look back at them, it's as if I'm saying, 'It might, and maybe you'll be okay. Just get there when you get there.'" —*Michael J. Fox, actor and founder of the Michael J. Fox Foundation for Parkinson's Research*

"I like to approach each subject with an open mind so I can listen and learn as much as possible and maybe even come away with an aha. I had a big one: The yearning to feel heard, needed, and important is so strong in all of us that we seek that validation in whatever form we can get it." —*Oprah*

"One day we broke into a recreation center stocked up with goodies . . . While we were in there eating as much as we could, I broke into an administrative room that had a piano in the corner. I almost closed the door, but something told me, Open that door, fool. And I did. I walked over and just put my finger over one piano key to see what sound it would make . . . Just like that, I heard music and felt a feeling I had never had in my life! . . . If I had closed that door, I might have had a whole 'nother life." —*Quincy Jones, musician*

"After many years of my weight going up and down—of saying on Monday 'I'm going to do it' and by Wednesday failing—I realized that the commitment to do well is a lifetime of choices that you make daily. The space to live in is not 'I'll try.' Not 'I want to.' It's 'I have decided.' . . . The click came as an emotional and spiritual awakening." —*Oprah*

"I can't inspire self-confidence in others if I personally haven't achieved it." —*Samantha Dunn, author*

"I had to get clear—about who I was and why it was okay to say no. I had to make others aware of my new limits, to resist the feeling that I was selfish because I took care of myself first. I learned to trust that my friends would still be my friends if I couldn't help them out financially. I learned that I would still be part of the family if I didn't go home for Christmas and that my lovers would still respect me when I stood my ground."
—*Shay Youngblood, author*

"A woman asked me, 'What was the aha light bulb moment in your life?' I realized it was when I figured out that my thoughts control my whole life—that no matter what hand life deals me, I can always choose my response to it . . . If you want your life to be more rewarding, you have to change the way you think."
—*Oprah*

"[In Mexico], I was making money, I was an actress, and I was famous. It looked like what I wanted, but it was not . . . It's what others would think that I'd want, and sometimes that makes you feel it's good enough. But is it your dream? And it wasn't my dream. And so I said that I'm going to leave it . . . I was excited about being brave about it and saying, 'What I left didn't grab me by the balls.' " —*Salma Hayek, actress*

"If you make a choice that goes against what everyone else thinks, the world doesn't fall apart." —*Oprah*

"Forget about kids: grown-ups say the darndest things. Sometimes they mean well, sometimes they mean to lacerate, sometimes they're just clueless. The challenge (at least for me) is not to take any of it personally . . . even when it's meant personally. Sticks and stones may break my bones, but words will never hurt me, unless of course I decide to let them." —*Lisa Kogan, writer*

"I no longer scramble blindly through hardship. I no longer emerge from a bad time feeling relieved just to have survived. Instead of despairing, I try to find the lesson within the experience." —*Halle Berry, actress*

"I was going through a divorce and my personal life was a mess . . . My friend Duke Ellington, who happened to be in town for a concert, had heard I was alone . . . I opened the door to find one of the greatest surprises of my life: there was a choir singing 'On a Clear Day You Can See Forever.' . . . For years this kindness from Duke lifted up my whole life. It showed me that no matter how bad things seem, there are always people in this world who care about others. That revelation changed my life." —*Tony Bennett, singer*

"Instead of waking up New Year's morning and saying, 'I'm going to do X now,' then berating yourself a month later when that resolution didn't work, remember: You're doing nothing less than rewiring your brain. Approach change as if you're learning a new language or new instrument. Obviously, you're not going to be fluent or play symphonies instantly; you'll need constant focus and practice." —*Rebecca Skloot, journalist*

"When we find ourselves waiting, whether through force of circumstance or lingering habit, we should listen deeply . . . We can learn to pervade the terrain of waiting with our awareness to make it vital, connected, and fully alive." —*Sharon Salzberg, meditation teacher*

"If you're trying in vain to quit something you do compulsively, like overspending or smoking or macramé, try quitting the effort to quit." —*Martha Beck, life coach*

"You won't be powerful in life until you are powerful over your money—how you feel about it, and how you treat it." —*Suze Orman, finance expert*

"Lying and cheating are sins. A hot fudge sundae is not." —*Tish Durkin, journalist*

"I've always wanted to be able to see where my life would take me, and now I understand that I can, because I know there is a direct connection between what I say and what happens to me." —*Jennifer Hudson, singer*

✳

"MORE THAN A DECADE AGO, MY STAFF AND I BOOKED A HUSBAND CAUGHT IN AN ADULTEROUS SEX SCANDAL, AND RIGHT THERE ON OUR STAGE BEFORE MILLIONS OF VIEWERS, THE WIFE HEARD THAT HER PARTNER HAD BEEN UNFAITHFUL. IT'S A MOMENT I HAVE NEVER FORGOTTEN: THE HUMILIATION AND DESPAIR ON THAT WOMAN'S FACE MADE ME ASHAMED FOR PUTTING HER IN THAT POSITION. RIGHT THEN, I DECIDED I'D NEVER AGAIN BE PART OF A SHOW THAT DEMEANS, EMBARRASSES, OR DIMINISHES ANOTHER HUMAN BEING . . . ONCE THE LIGHT BULB CAME ON FOR ME THAT DAY, MY CALLING BECAME TO CREATE SHOWS THAT ENCOURAGE AND INSPIRE AS MUCH AS THEY ENTERTAIN—TELEVISION THAT LEAVES GUESTS WITH THEIR DIGNITY AND HELPS US ALL SEE OUR LIVES IN A DIFFERENT WAY." —OPRAH

FINDING
YOUR BALANCE

✳

I'VE LEARNED THAT YOU CAN'T
HAVE EVERYTHING AND DO EVERYTHING
AT THE SAME TIME.

—OPRAH

"Solitude is the soul's holiday, an opportunity to stop doing for others and to surprise and delight ourselves instead . . . In solitude, we discover what makes us feel alive."
—*Katrina Kenison, author*

"He who cannot rest cannot work; he who cannot let go cannot hold on . . ." —*Harry Emerson Fosdick, clergyman*

"To do nothing at all is the most difficult thing in the world, the most difficult and the most intellectual." —*Oscar Wilde, playwright*

"As we look deeply within, we understand our perfect balance. There is no fear of the cycle of birth, life, and death. For when you stand in the present moment, you are timeless." —*Rodney Yee, yoga teacher*

"None of us is built to run nonstop. That's why, when you don't give yourself the time and care you need, your body rebels in the form of sickness and exhaustion. How do I give back to myself? Hardly a day goes by that I don't talk things out with my best friend, Gayle, who is usually interested in every detail—we call it book, chapter, and verse." —*Oprah*

"I can tell you with absolute assurance that it is impossible for women to achieve the kind of balance recommended by many well-meaning self-help counselors . . . My conclusion? Balance schmalance. Trying to establish a harmonious equilibrium between our society's definitions of What a Woman Should Be is like trying to resolve the tensions between two hostile enemies by locking them in a room together." —*Martha Beck, life coach*

"We can be sure that the greatest hope for maintaining equilibrium in the face of any situation rests within ourselves."
—*Francis J. Braceland, psychiatrist*

"Every time you say no to a less-than-appealing request, you say yes to something else. Maybe it's one golden hour to take a bubble bath, read a good book, or play with your kids. Saying no frees you to pursue a dream—to take a class and develop your potential, or to work for a cause you believe in. The more time you can give to the things you truly care about, the more satisfying your life will feel." —*Connie Hatch, author*

"Learning to delegate and finding the strength to say no are two of the hardest and most emotionally complex time management skills. Guilt, perfectionism, and the fear of imposing on other people keep us from sharing the burden. Yet when we can actually see the real and measurable limits of our time, ambivalence about embracing these two skills disappears."
—*Julie Morgenstern, organization expert*

"When people come to me and say, 'I want to be just like you; the only thing I want in life is to sing,' I tell them this: 'Please don't make your career your life.' Let it be your passion, let it bring pleasure, but don't let it become your identity. You are so much more valuable than that." —*Celine Dion, singer*

"We can't take a recess from life—it keeps going on. But we can take recesses from feeling trapped anytime. If you take a deep breath and look around, 'Look what's happening to me!' can become 'Look what's happening!' And what's happening? The incredible drama of life is happening. And we're in it! What's going to happen? Who knows? You can feel your body, alive, breathing, and use all your senses to connect you to the present moment. Moments of connection are free moments—Tahitis of the mind." —*Sylvia Boorstein, psychologist*

"What I know for sure is this: You are built not to shrink down to less, but to blossom into more. To be more splendid. To be more extraordinary. To use every moment to fill yourself up." —*Oprah*

"When we finally learn that self-care begins and ends with ourselves, we no longer demand sustenance and happiness from others." —*Jennifer Louden, author*

"You must have a room, or a certain hour or so a day, where you don't know what was in the newspapers that morning . . . a place where you can simply experience and bring forth what you are and what you might be." —*Joseph Campbell, mythologist*

"All you need are sneakers. When you feel better, you act better, you have a better outlook, and you eat better. I'm the one who says, 'Just one more mile. Let's just go around the next corner.' I love the way it feels. It's exercise that lets me do everything else—that's where I get my strength from, knowing I can do it." —*Jo Shenk, marathon runner and double mastectomy survivor*

"Every challenge we take on has the power to shake us—to knock us to our knees. And yet what's even more disconcerting than the jolt itself is our fear that we won't withstand it. When we feel the ground beneath us shifting, we panic . . . What I know for sure is that the only way to endure the quake is to shift your stance." —*Oprah*

"When life demands so much of us—not just the responsibilities of adulthood but the speed and resilience of eternal adolescence—reading may be a necessary escape. It may be what makes the practical day, with its dishwashing and shoe tying, its clock ticking out our deficiencies and our mortality, not just bearable but embraceable." —*Pamela Erens, writer*

"If you peel back the layers of your life—the frenzy, the noise—stillness is waiting. That stillness is you." —*Oprah*

"People who are unhappy in their lives rarely take a deep breath. They don't sleep well, don't eat right, and carry tensions in their bodies. If you're overweight or feeling burdened by endless stress, your body is telling you something. It's time to start listening." —*Phil McGraw, psychologist*

"I had to hit burnout more than once before I understood the wisdom of balance—of coming back to my center for rejuvenation. For me, that now comes once a week on Sundays, when I clear both my schedule and my head to regather myself. If you neglect to charge a battery, it dies. And if you run full-speed ahead without stopping for water, you lose momentum to finish the race." —*Oprah*

"I have this job that I love, but I'm also like, When can I go home? In a way, that's good, because otherwise, I'd never go home. I would just kill myself doing this show."
—*Tina Fey, comedian*

"The biggest reason I have so much endurance is because I do what *I* want to do. I stopped trying to please other people. The other day I did something because someone else wanted me to and I was exhausted. Why? Because the intention was wrong."
—*Oprah*

"The artist knows he must be alone to create; the writer, to work out his thoughts; the musician, to compose; the saint, to pray. But women need solitude in order to find again the true essence of themselves." —*Anne Morrow Lindbergh, aviation pioneer and author*

✳

"I'VE LEARNED THAT YOU CAN'T HAVE EVERYTHING AND DO EVERYTHING AT THE SAME TIME. I HOPE YOU'LL TELL YOURSELF THE TRUTH ABOUT WHAT MATTERS MOST TO YOU, KNOW THAT YOUR HOURS IN THIS LIFE ARE LIMITED FOR ATTAINING IT—THEN DECIDE HOW YOU'LL USE YOUR MOST PRECIOUS RESOURCE." —OPRAH

SPIRITUALITY: YOUR THOUGHTS AND BELIEFS

SPIRITUALITY FOR ME IS
RECOGNIZING THAT I AM CONNECTED TO
THE ENERGY OF ALL CREATION.

—OPRAH

"The word *religion* derives from the Latin word *religare*, whic
means 'to bind together' . . . As you go along your spiritu
search, observe the long-term effect of every doctrine a
practice that comes your way. If it breaks, shatters, or destr
it's not religion—it's absolutism. That drug'll kill you.
religion, by definition, makes things whole again. It h
—*Martha Beck, life coach*

"Living in the present does not mean surrendering our responsibility to correct some things from the past or to plan and make way for the future; in fact, it is the ultimate taking of responsibility for both. The only point where God's time—eternity—meets time as we know it is in the present moment. And in that place of power, both past and future are healed."
—*Marianne Williamson, spiritual teacher*

"Faith can give us the courage to face the uncertainties of the future." —*Martin Luther King Jr., civil rights leader and Nobel Peace Prize recipient*

"Conventional wisdom says the opposite of faith is doubt. But doubt, applied in the right way—as curiosity and a willingness to question—can enrich and enliven our faith."
—*Sharon Salzberg, meditation teacher*

"What you risk reveals what you value." —*Jeanette Winterson, novelist*

"Your thoughts are not who you are. They're not reality. You can have all sorts of concepts of water, but they can't quench your thirst. Thoughts are not the truth. If you can recognize that, your thoughts have less power over you; you can let them go." —*Tara Brach, psychologist*

"If there is an ever after—please, please, please—I would be leaving part of my family, but I can go and join another part, and wait for that day when we're all together again. In some ways, it's something you yearn for . . . a relief."
—*Elizabeth Edwards, lawyer, cancer survivor, and former wife of politician John Edwards*

"Every day the path to your own spirituality starts with clarifying who you are and what you want. Not just *things*—things are easy. I mean the stuff that really matters. Life isn't just about what you can have; it's about what you have to give. What kind of person do you really want to be?" —*Oprah*

"I write fiction mostly to try to make sense of my own petty and profound misery, and I fail every time, but every time, I come away with a peculiar sort of contentment, as if it was just the trying that mattered. And maybe that's the best answer to the patently ridiculous problem of trying to reconcile all the very visible evil and suffering in the world with the existence of a God who is not actually out to get us: we suffer and we don't give up." —*Chris Adrian, medical doctor and author*

"Faith is not something to grasp, it is a state to grow into."
—*Mahatma Gandhi, former political and spiritual leader of India*

"Intention is not just about will—or about resolutions we make on New Year's Eve with shaky hope in our hearts—but about our overall everyday vision, what we long for, what we believe is possible for us. If we want to know the spirit of our activities, the emotional tone of our efforts, we have to look at our intentions." —*Sharon Salzberg, meditation teacher*

"What you believe has more power than what you dream or wish or hope for. You become what you believe." —*Oprah*

"Back of every creation, supporting it like an arch, is faith. Enthusiasm is nothing; it comes and goes. But if one believes, then miracles occur." —*Henry Miller, novelist and painter*

"Now faith is the substance of things hoped for, the evidence of things not seen." —*Hebrews 11:1*

"We don't know all the reasons that propel us on a spiritual journey, but somehow our life compels us to go. Something in us knows that we are not just here to toil at our work. There is a mysterious pull to remember." —*Jack Kornfield, Buddhist teacher*

"What you find in your mind is what you put there. Put good things in there." —*Ron Rathbun, meditation teacher*

"Human beings are unbelievably strong and terribly hopeful about what's going to happen next. Though everyone's faith is different, I've seen that people have faith in goodness. And whenever they get to the end of life, that goodness takes over. They believe that when they leave this world, a peace will come." —*Julie Freischlag, surgeon*

"Faith is the highest passion in a human being. Many in every generation may not come that far, but none comes further." —*Søren Kierkegaard, theologian*

"I grew up with the idea that everything we are is in response to what was done to us . . . [yet] so many preferences we believe to be intellectually driven have nothing to do with what we think but rather with what we feel." —*Rachel Griffiths, actress*

"My image of God may not be the personal God so many pray to. But, yes, I do believe in the everyday preciousness of life. That is what I call God. But faith. Do I have faith? . . . I have faith that it's not what you believe but how you live your life that matters. I have faith in my ability to love and be loved . . . Most important, I have faith that helping other people is the true key to fulfillment. Certainly to mine." —*Sally Quinn, journalist*

"We doctors never really know why one patient gets better while another dies. So, like primitive animals, we often go about our business along the same well-worn rut. We are scientists, sure—but when the chips are down, we're never too far from rubbing a rabbit's foot." —*Kent Sepkowitz, medical doctor*

"Faith is the response of the soul to the divine thrust toward perfection, toward great, more perfect wholes." —*Rabbi Jacob B. Agus, theologian*

"Faith, among the faithful I know, is not about perfection. It's about knowing, as Quakers would put it, that there is an inextinguishable light inside everyone that is holy. It's about valuing the holy in the face of the flawed, about leaving room to grow, to fall down, then to get back up again, all with equal dignity. And so, I find after a year of practicing, is a good marriage." —*Lise Funderburg, writer*

"We have so little tolerance for uncomfortable feelings. I'm not even talking about unpleasant outer circumstances, but that feeling in your stomach of I don't want this to be happening. You try to escape it in some way, but if somehow you could stay present and touch the rawness of the experience, you can really learn something." —*Pema Chödrön, Buddhist nun*

"I was talking with my nine-year-old daughter last night about what's waiting for us on the other side of life. She's old enough now to get as mystified and misty-eyed about these things as I do. I told her I believe that when people die, their love-energy and goodwill can stay with us. That faith is wonderfully comforting." —*Diane Lane, actress*

"I meditate twice a day for half an hour. In meditation, I can let go of everything. I'm not Hugh Jackman. I'm not a dad. I'm not a husband. I'm just dipping into that powerful source that creates everything. I take a little bath in it." —*Hugh Jackman, actor*

"I've found that in having a child, you're confronted by your mortality each day as the child grows and blossoms. But every single element in our Western society is in denial of death. We don't want to think about it, which compounds the terror we feel about it." —*Cate Blanchett, actress*

"Can one be spiritual without religious faith? One can. All one needs is to be open to someone else's concerns, fears, and hopes, and to make him or her feel less alone . . . It is my caring for the otherness of the other that determines humanity. And my spirituality." —*Elie Wiesel, Holocaust survivor and Nobel Peace Prize recipient*

"Everyone has what I call an SPS—a Spiritual Positioning System—to guide them. This SPS is the instinct that makes you stop multitasking and lean in closer to hear what someone's saying because a sentence suddenly gives you the chills . . . It's the headline that stays in your mind long after it fades from the TV screen, prompting you to think, Do I have a talent or idea that could turn this problem into yesterday's news? . . . Is there someone I forgot I wanted to be? As long as you keep letting life ask you another question—and reveal that there is always more for you to be and do—you are unstoppable."
—*Alice Sebold, author*

"The big miracles we're waiting on are happening right in front of us, at every moment, with every breath. Open your eyes and heart and you'll begin to see them." —*Oprah*

"Faith helps us approach life with a sense of possibility rather than foreboding and helplessness. It dares us to imagine what we might be capable of. It enables us to reach for what we don't yet know with a measure of courage. It gives us resilience in times of difficulty, and the ability to respond to challenges without feeling trapped. My own faith has taught me that whatever disappointments I might meet, I can try again, trust again, and love again." —*Sharon Salzberg, meditation teacher*

"I can recognize the divine in my own daily life, that unexpected shift I sometimes get while listening to music, dancing, chopping vegetables, even walking home from the subway when the light is just right. In those moments, I feel linked to a stillness so unlike the rat-a-tat of my usual thoughts and worries." —*Kendra Hurley, writer*

"If you do not know where you stand within yourself, where does that leave you? When you stand centered in your own space, it will become clearer what your choices are and which ones to make." —*Ron Rathbun, meditation teacher*

"You need time with yourself, not a friend or a man. When you sit with yourself, you can't ignore your thoughts and feelings. You may have to go through pain, but on the other side is the good stuff. You don't have to be afraid of being alone." —*Eileen Fisher, clothing designer*

"Life is consciousness." —*Emmet Fox, spiritual leader*

"A woman cannot directly choose her circumstances, but she can choose her thoughts, and so indirectly, yet surely, shape her circumstance . . . As a woman thinketh in her heart, so is she." —*Dorothy Hulst, author*

"I once passed a billboard that caught my attention. It read, 'He who dies with the most toys is still dead.' Anyone who has ever come close to death can tell you that at the end of your life, you probably won't be reminiscing about how many all-nighters you pulled at the office or how much your mutual fund is worth. The thoughts that linger are the 'if only' questions, like Who could I have become if I had finally done the things I always wanted to do?" —*Oprah*

"Knowing the extent of our limitation, feeling our soon-not-to-be-here-ness in our bones, is the best condition we can have for waking up to the miracle that we are here now at all . . . That is the brilliance of the human design plan: the built-in 'defect' is the very thing that can spur us to drink down the full draft as it comes to us. Better to taste it now, this life that we have, than to defer it to some future that may never come."
—*Roger Housden, author*

"Death is not the biggest fear we have; our biggest fear is taking the risk to be alive and to express what we really are. We have learned to live our lives trying to satisfy other people's demands. We have learned to live by other people's points of view because of the fear of not being accepted."
—*Don Miguel Ruiz, author*

"We spend our lives avoiding the situations that help us grow. It's when we stay with uncertainty and discomfort without trying to fix it that we connect with our own innate joy, wisdom, and love." —*Pema Chödrön, Buddhist nun*

"Until you make peace with who you are, you'll never be content with what you have." —*Doris Mortman, author*

"Faith is a mystery; it is a journey without a map. It unfolds like a rose, sometimes tightly budded, sometimes in full bloom. When you think it has withered, it sprouts somewhere else. When you think you've got it figured out, you discover a deeper layer or a path you never knew existed. I once was lost but now I'm found. Amazing grace." —*Sue Irsfeld, editor*

"On the way to work each morning, I look for something new on every block. On the first block, I check out the window of the Ralph Lauren store to see if the display has changed. On the second block, it's the Crate & Barrel window. On the third block, I look for the paperboy. What is he wearing today? And so on. This little game helps me to tune in rather than zone out, to stay conscious rather than move unconsciously through the day and, ultimately, through life." —*Oprah*

"In the word *question*, there is a beautiful word—*quest*. I love that word. We are all partners in a quest. The essential questions have no answers. You are my question and I am yours—and then there is a dialogue." —*Elie Wiesel, Holocaust survivor and Nobel Peace Prize recipient*

"When you see with reverence, you see holiness in everything. Holiness is like the ocean. What you see with your five senses is like the wave in the ocean. There are so many waves that you will never see them all . . . All of them change in their own ways and disappear into the ocean in their own ways. Each one is unique. Reverence is loving the ocean." —*Gary Zukav, author and spiritual teacher*

"The practice of lovingkindness meditation brings to life our innate capacity for connecting to ourselves and others. The lovingkindness we cultivate breaks the habit of indifference or judgment that keeps us feeling separate from others. A capacity for friendship and kindness exists within each of us, without exception. No matter what pain we might have gone through in our lives, that capacity is never destroyed. It may be—and often is—obscured, but it's there." —*Sharon Salzberg, meditation teacher*

"Your life is a multipart series of all your experiences—and each experience is created by your thoughts, intention, and actions to teach you what you most need to know. Your life is a journey of learning to love yourself first and then extending that love to others in every encounter. How can you travel on that road without fear? Whenever I'm faced with a difficult decision, I ask myself, What would I do if I weren't afraid of making a mistake, feeling rejected, or being alone? Remove the fear, and the answer comes into focus."
—*Oprah*

"Just as the purpose of a plant is to grow, so it is that the main purpose of every human being is to survive and to grow until death. As far as mental development is concerned, we should *never* be complacent. We can develop our minds infinitely—there is no limitation." —*Fourteenth Dalai Lama, Buddhist leader*

"Realize deeply that the present moment is all you ever have."
—*Eckhart Tolle, spiritual teacher*

"What lies behind us and what lies before us are tiny matters compared to what lies within us." —*Ralph Waldo Emerson, philosopher*

"You cannot control the world outside, but you can choose what you will bring into yourself. If you do not see anything of value in life, begin by finding one thing of beauty every day until it becomes a habit." —*Ron Rathbun, meditation teacher*

"I do believe it is possible to create, even without ever writing a word or painting a picture, by simply molding one's inner life. And that too is a deed." —*Etty Hillesum, writer*

"Financial freedom is not about having money. You are never free until you have power over how you think and feel about your money and how you invest and spend it." —*Suze Orman, finance expert*

"Failures can be God's little whispers; other times, they are full earthquakes erupting in our lives because we didn't listen to the whispers. Failure is just a way for our lives to show us that we are moving in the wrong direction, that we should try something different. It holds no more power than we give it." —*Oprah*

"If you can solve your problem, then what is the need of worrying? If you cannot solve it, then what is the use of worrying?" —*Shantideva, Buddhist scholar*

"You create your thoughts, and your thoughts create your life. Do you like what you have created? Contemplate yourself each day and you will unravel the mystery of not only what you are but who you are." —*Ron Rathbun, meditation teacher*

✳

"SPIRITUALITY FOR ME IS RECOGNIZING THAT I AM CONNECTED TO THE ENERGY OF ALL CREATION, THAT I AM PART OF IT—AND IT IS ALWAYS A PART OF ME . . . ALLOWING THE TRUTH OF WHO YOU ARE—YOUR SPIRITUAL SELF—TO RULE YOUR LIFE MEANS YOU STOP THE STRUGGLE AND LEARN TO MOVE WITH THE FLOW OF YOUR LIFE." —OPRAH

AGING BRILLIANTLY

✳

IF IT'S TRUE WHAT MAYA ANGELOU SAYS—
THAT THE FIFTIES REPRESENT EVERYTHING YOU
WERE MEANT TO BE—ALL I CAN SAY
IS WATCH OUT.

—OPRAH

"When I was twenty-six, I didn't know who I was. And at thirty-six, I didn't know who I was. Now I do. I think that's what being authentic is—when you finally know you."
—*Jamie Lee Curtis, actress*

"The person who has lived the most is not the one with the most years but the one with the richest experiences."
—*Jean-Jacques Rousseau, philosopher*

"Before I turned forty, I thought I would be concerned about aging, but I'm not. My gray hair came about because I went scuba diving with my eldest daughter, Erika. Prior to our dive, I'd been using a semipermanent dye. So when I went down in that ocean and came back up, this hair was gray . . . I looked at myself and said, 'Oh my God, it's time for me to accept this.' I was about forty-two. That is part of the honesty, the honesty of my age and what is attendant with aging."
—*Camille Cosby, philanthropist and wife of comedian Bill Cosby*

"In my late fifties, I began to embrace myself in a way that I hadn't been able to before. I find that I'm not as worried about what other people think. That's a comfortable place to be. And I'm starting to let go of the feeling that I need to push myself to do things I don't want to do." —*Sally Field, actress*

"I feel guilty about doing nothing, but as I get older, that's all I really want to do. For so many years, I was doing exactly what I was supposed to be doing as an enlightened, cultured person. I used to go to the ballet thirty times a year. Now I think, Do I really want to schlep all the way there? I want to stay home, pet my dog . . . and watch *Law & Order*."
—*Isaac Mizrahi, clothing designer*

"Once a competitor, always a competitor. Everyone assumes that as you age your feelings of competitiveness dissipate, but they don't. People my age and older have been telling me they are going to do something they have never done before. I love that." —*Dara Torres, oldest medalist in Olympic swimming history*

"Today I am sixty-five years old. I still look good. I appreciate and enjoy my age . . . A lot of people resist transition and therefore never allow themselves to enjoy who they are. Embrace the change, no matter what it is; once you do, you can learn about the new world you're in and take advantage of it. You still bring to bear all your prior experience, but you're riding on another level. It's completely liberating." —*Nikki Giovanni, poet*

"There's a saying, 'Life makes you ready to meet with the things you meet with.' At sixty-seven I can deal with things that would have completely devastated me at thirty-three. Like the death of a friend. The person who's going to deal with Alzheimer's is not the thirty-three-year-old you. The person who's going to deal with Alzheimer's is a person who has built courage and tenacity . . . We build strength, disappointment by disappointment." —*Rachel Naomi Remen, medical doctor*

"Getting older is the best thing that ever happened to me. I wake up every morning rejoicing that I'm still here with the opportunity to begin again and be better." —*Oprah*

"There's a reason why forty, fifty, and sixty don't look the way they used to, and it's not because of feminism or better living through exercise. It's because of hair dye. In the 1950s, only 7 percent of American women dyed their hair; today there are parts of Manhattan and Los Angeles where there are no gray-haired women at all." —*Nora Ephron, writer*

"Becoming a bag lady. Getting Alzheimer's. Ending up alone. All of these concerns speak to a fear not of aging but of living. What is a fear of living? It's being preeminently afraid of dying. It is not doing what you came here to do, out of timidity and spinelessness. The antidote is to take full responsibility for yourself—for the time you take up and the space you occupy. If you don't know what you're here to do, then just do some good." —*Maya Angelou, author*

"It is a mistake to regard age as a downhill grade toward dissolution. The reverse is true. As one grows older, one climbs with surprising strides." —*George Sand, author*

"The wrinkles and the double chin are smoke screens for what we're really afraid of—mortality. I happen to believe that our souls continue after we're gone, and that makes life on earth less fearful. We're here for a reason, and challenges are handed to us so we can grow and become more of who we're meant to be. So I deal with my fear of aging and death by making it my spiritual practice. Not turning away from it, not pretending it doesn't exist, not slapping on a cosmetic Band-Aid. But by taking on a fearless attitude toward what really is happening to my body and my life."
—*Elizabeth Lesser, author*

"The surface, the superficial, the way one looks has become valued too highly in our society. When the skin begins to sag, many women go for Botox. Why on earth would you let somebody stick a needle in your face just to get rid of a wrinkle? Here's the real question: What do we have to do to place more value on age? We have to value ourselves not for what we look like or the things we possess, but for the women we are."
—*Maya Angelou, author*

"There is no old age. There is, as there always was, just you."
—*Carol Matthau, writer*

"I wouldn't even go back to as young as I was yesterday. Being this age is completely freeing. To walk out of the house without wondering who's looking back at you makes it possible to focus on what you really want to focus on. It makes it possible to get your work done." —*Abigail Thomas, writer*

"I am more myself and more at home in myself today than I was at twenty or even fifty. You can see this in my eyes. In fact, you can see all the ages I've been in my eyes, and if you look really hard, you can even see my secret, which is the knowledge that vitality, wisdom, humor—the intangible we call 'soul'—survives when superficial beauty fades. That's a powerful secret, and if it turns heads, it's because young people who may not understand themselves might be hypnotized by people who do." —*Linda Ellerbee, writer*

"In my head, I think I'm thirty-eight on a good day, and hanging in around forty-two on my slowest day. No matter, I know the number is irrelevant. It's what you decide to do with it that matters." —*Oprah*

"You grow up the first day you have your first real laugh—at yourself." —*Ethel Barrymore, actress*

"Whatever your calendar age, by recalling a passionate encounter, you reawaken the vitality of adolescence, without the acne . . . It's often why my single clients finally hook up with the man or the woman of their dreams . . . We think that attracting the right person will make us feel young, but really, it's feeling young that helps us attract the right person."
—*Martha Beck, life coach*

"To mature is in part to realize that while complete intimacy and omniscience and power cannot be had, self-transcendence, growth, and closeness to others are nevertheless within one's reach." —*Sissela Bok, philosopher*

"I wish I could tell you that sex gets better as we get older, I really do. But as you probably know if you're already there, the postmenopausal orgasm can be a very elusive character . . . So: Better, no. Different, yes. More loving, if less urgent, yes. More complex and compassionate, yes."
—*Valerie Monroe, writer*

"The practice of maturing is an art to be learned, an effort to be sustained. By the age of fifty, you have made yourself what you are, and if it is good, it is better than your youth."
—*Marya Mannes, journalist*

"At my age . . . I'm going to do what I want and I haven't got time for anything else." —*Florynce Kennedy, lawyer*

"There are years that ask questions and years that answer." —*Zora Neale Hurston, author*

"I feel about aging the way William Saroyan said he felt about death: Everybody has to do it, but I always believed an exception would be made in my case." —*Martha Beck, life coach*

"Women may be the one group that grows more radical with age." —*Gloria Steinem, women's rights activist*

"I've turned forty-two. I can bench-press all I want and gravity will still take its toll. My skin will continue to lose its elasticity. My metabolism will continue to slow. But this fitness I have now is not about recapturing the sheen of youth. It's about rediscovering a time from my early life when the body was in service to the spirit, when it was an expression of drive and joy and grace without all the filters of what women should and can't look like. I feel power and freedom I haven't known since I was a girl. And that allows me to know myself better as a woman." —*Lise Funderburg, writer*

"Whether you're twenty-eight or eighty-eight, you've probably stamped yourself with a label. Look at the label that comes with your age, then replace it with the one that reflects the reality of your life. I know for sure that every birthday, you decide whether to mark it the end of your greatest days or the beginning of your finest hour. Your call."
—*Oprah*

"Age has given me what I was looking for my entire life— it gave me me. It provided the time and experience and failures and triumphs and friends who helped me step into the shape that had been waiting for me all my life."
—*Anne Lamott, writer*

"I think most of us become nicer as we get older, less judgmental, less full of certitude; life tends to knock a few corners off all of us as we go through. Cancer, divorce, teenagers, and other plagues make us give up on expecting ourselves—or life—to be perfect, which is a real relief."
—*Molly Ivins, writer*

"I never lose sight of the fact that just being is fun."
—*Katharine Hepburn, actress*

"Getting there isn't half the fun—it's all the fun."

—*Robert Townsend, former chairman of Avis*

"I became more successful in my mid-forties, but that pales compared to the other gifts of this decade—how kind to myself I have become, what a wonderful, tender wife I am to myself, what a loving companion. I get myself tubs of hot salty water at the end of the day in which to soak my tired feet. I run interference for myself when I am working, like the wife of a great artist would: 'No, I'm sorry, she can't come. She's working hard these days and needs a lot of downtime.' I live by the truth that *No* is a complete sentence. I rest as a spiritual act."

—*Anne Lamott, writer*

"At forty—was it the biochemical boost, the being done with babies, the power of my newfound wisdom, the long-awaited spare cash, the calmer, gentler marriage, or (hello!) all of the above?—I felt a renewal of passion. I began to write another novel, a sensual story that thrilled me to work on. I thought about things I hadn't allowed myself to: traveling to Italy, lightening my hair. I bought a pen at Tiffany's because now that I was forty, damn it, I deserved one."

—*Cathi Hanauer, writer*

"To keep the heart unwrinkled, to be hopeful, kindly, cheerful, reverent—that is to triumph over old age."
—*Thomas Bailey Aldrich, writer*

"Charm doesn't fade, wit doesn't age, and knowledge is still priceless. If we live well, every year we become a year's worth better, smarter, and wiser. Good humor is more attractive than good breasts, and I think fudge and pets are better than sex. Cheer up and enjoy today, because it will get worse."
—*Molly Ivins, writer*

"This is the best time in my life—the first eighty years are definitely the hardest." —*Carol Channing, actress*

"To be seventy years young is sometimes far more cheerful and hopeful than to be forty years old." —*Oliver Wendell Holmes Sr., poet*

"You can only perceive real beauty in a person as they get older." —*Anouk Aimée, actress*

"The great secret that all old people share is that you really haven't changed in seventy or eighty years. Your body changes, but you don't change at all." —*Doris Lessing, novelist*

"The seventies are hot." —*Maya Angelou, author*

"To Thirtysomething Me, my body was my enemy. But Old Me looked wistfully at this body—this young, able, healthy, juicy body. 'Are you crazy?' is how she expressed herself. 'You know it's all downhill from here.' And then she faded back into the future, leaving me with the understanding that a smart person would appreciate this body for the marvel that it is. I don't think I've said a mean word to it since, though occasionally I've had to bite my tongue (gently)." —*Amy Gross, editor and writer*

"I believe the older you get, the more access you have to real fun: You know what makes you happy, which isn't necessarily what you once thought it would be. In every moment, you have the ability to choose what serves your best interest and will bring you the most fun. Why not do it now?" —*Oprah*

"Most of us get to a certain stage in life—maybe it happens when you're fifty-four, like me—when you come to terms with who you are, what your talents are, and what your shortcomings are . . . I am confident that I'll be able to do a good job at what I know." —*Laura Bush, former First Lady*

"If I could trade being older and wiser for being young and wise, I would, but I don't see that as an option. I see glorious young women striding down the street and recognize their expression of displeasure, their self-consciousness and discontent. They're perfect and they don't know it because they can't. The irony of this cracks me up, for which I'm unaccountably grateful." —*Karen Karbo, writer*

"I think about when we get old, but I can't imagine life without Oprah. I really can't. I'll go first if I can be ninety and [she] can be ninety-one." —*Gayle King, editor*

✳

"ALL THESE YEARS I'VE BEEN TAKING LESSONS FROM LIFE EXPERIENCES AND FEELING LIKE I WAS GROWING INTO MYSELF. FINALLY, I FEEL GROWN. MORE LIKE MYSELF THAN I'VE EVER BEEN. IF IT'S TRUE WHAT MAYA ANGELOU SAYS—THAT THE FIFTIES REPRESENT EVERYTHING YOU WERE MEANT TO BE—ALL I CAN SAY IS WATCH OUT."
—OPRAH

REINVENTING
YOURSELF WITH
BOLDNESS

✳

I HAVE CREATED A LIFE BY STEPPING

OUT OF THE BOX OF PEOPLE'S LIMITATIONS.

I CALL IT ZIGGING WHEN OTHERS ARE ZAGGING.

—OPRAH

"Sometimes you have to make your own opportunities, and that's why I'm on TV. I wasn't going to sit around anymore, waiting for the damn phone to ring. I had to create my own place—I've always done that." —*Bette Midler, actress*

"Growth and self-transformation cannot be delegated."
—*Lewis Mumford, architectural critic*

"Many of us have spent a lifetime trying to be what we're not, feeling lousy about ourselves when we fail, and sometimes even when we succeed. We hide our differences when, by accepting and celebrating them, we could collaborate to make every effort more exciting, productive, enjoyable, and powerful. Personally, I think we should start right now."
—*Martha Beck, life coach*

"Let the world know you as you are, not as you think you should be, because sooner or later, if you are posing, you will forget the pose, and then where are you?" —*Fanny Brice, actress*

"I think it was playwright Jane Wagner who said, 'All my life I wanted to be *somebody*, but I see now I should've been more specific.'" —*Oprah*

"Getting started, keeping going, getting started again—in art and in life, it seems to me this is the essential rhythm."
—*Seamus Heaney, poet*

"There is no insurance policy in life—and no guarantee you'll always make all the best decisions. But that's all right. Bottom line: Give yourself permission to call your own shots, even if you may be wrong." —*Phil McGraw, psychologist*

"I know for sure that while it's great to have role models, we should never try to be anyone but ourselves."
—*Mattie J. T. Stepanek, poet who died from muscular dystrophy at age fourteen*

"Women have skills that we don't even know we have. You've got to learn to reinvent yourself. Write 'new' on the box. Never be complacent. Stay ready to go to the next step. Think the way Americans thought in the early days of our nation: we are entrepreneurs, grasping opportunity, unafraid of rejection. We've got to get into the habit of constantly learning something new." —*Joan Hamburg, radio host*

"You need only to claim the events of your life to make yourself yours. When you truly possess all you have been and done, which may take some time, you are fierce with reality."
—*Florida Pier Scott-Maxwell, writer*

"Whatever someone did to you in the past has no power over the present." —*Oprah*

"My future starts when I wake up every morning . . . Every day I find something creative to do with my life." —*Miles Davis, jazz musician*

"Sure, it's possible to pull out of a [career] stall. But it requires nothing short of a personal reinvention. You must take full responsibility for what has happened to your career, relieving all others of blame. And at the same time, you must push your performance to new heights, delivering outsize results with an unrelenting, upbeat attitude. Sound hard? It is . . . So leave you must, difficult as that surely sounds." —*Suzy Welch, writer*

"Because of cancer, I have certain things I never wanted: an ID card in my wallet from the Dana-Farber Cancer Institute, a 'chemo perm' that has turned my once very manageable straight hair into a toilet brush of coarse, unruly curls, and a slight aversion to the pleasant shade of lilac that hospitals use to denote cytotoxic medical waste. But I also have one less thing to be afraid of." —*Geraldine Brooks, journalist*

"Making the absolute best of ourselves is not an easy task. It is a pleasurable pursuit . . . but it requires patience, persistence, and perseverance." —*Sarah Ban Breathnach, author*

"It's not true that 'there is nothing new under the sun': There has never been, and never will be, anyone who sees, thinks, or responds exactly the way you do. Whether you're revolutionizing physics or making a quilt, you must display your differences to make a difference." —*Martha Beck, life coach*

"Know this: If you are following your own moral rules, the very things you're ashamed of are likely the things about which you can feel most proud. Say you've battled obesity, mental illness, addiction, or abuse: take pride in the extraordinary courage you've shown by surviving and working toward health. If others make you feel ashamed for what you are— your heritage, your sense of what is true for you—you'll find that expressing pride in those same qualities is the road to inner peace." —*Martha Beck, life coach*

"People often ask me, 'How do you do the same show over and over again?' But we do the same routine in life over and over again. People have the same relationships. We go through the same patterns. My acting teacher once said, 'Acting is the best training for life.' I have the opportunity to do the same show, but to make it deeper each time. And isn't that what we're here for?" —*Hugh Jackman, actor*

"You never know what you can do before you try it. And each time you go out, it's an experiment, a work in progress. You learn an awful lot about yourself—about your limits, your endurance, your capabilities . . . I think that everybody has a certain level of fear. The question is how we manage it. And I have managed to be able to control it enough in order to do my job." —*Christiane Amanpour, international correspondent*

"I don't know whether addiction is principally genetic, a result of emotional injury, or a combination of both. But all that matters is what I do today. Insight doesn't cure the addict any more than insight cures diabetes. You may understand perfectly well how diabetes works, but if you don't take your insulin, you're dead. The same is true with addiction. It doesn't matter what got you there; it's how you conduct yourself today, day by day." —*Bobby Kennedy Jr., environmental lawyer*

"After college, I bartended while working for the state on a puppet show about disabilities—I was literally helping and hurting people, all on the same day. While the show was a noble effort, it was completely unsatisfying because I didn't feel part of it. When I dreamed, I dreamed of being somebody else. I realized I needed to create something I felt part of. Then slowly, that feeling of wanting to be something else went away."
—*Jon Stewart, political satirist*

"I have pursued life on my own terms, changing my mind continuously about everything under the sun from sex to faith to ideology to ideals." —*Liz Smith, columnist*

"To let yourself be carried on passively is unthinkable."
—*Virginia Woolf, writer*

"The foundation of a financial fresh start actually has nothing to do with money or specific financial dos and don'ts. The first, and most difficult, step is to absolve yourself and your spouse or partner of any guilt. So you need to make a promise to me: I need you to agree that the past is past, and we are going to focus on the future . . . We are free to move forward only when we remove the emotional shackles of regret."

—*Suze Orman, finance expert*

"Man's main task is to give birth to himself."

—*Erich Fromm, social psychologist*

"Right now, make a list of what you admire about yourself—don't stop until you've filled a page. Sit and relish each quality and accomplishment. When you remember how much you have to be proud of, you don't need to envy others. Instead of wallowing in your jealousy, use your friends' accomplishments as inspiration to pursue the life *you* want."

—*Phil McGraw, psychologist*

"I received a note from a friend with this wise saying: 'Every time a heart cracks . . . somewhere, something beautiful is being born.' I look forward to the rebirthing." —*Oprah*

"I'm very aware that I'm different. I'm very aware that I don't fit in and that I'm not going along with the rules . . . I understand that I'm being truthful to who I am, and not too many people can say that." —*Ellen DeGeneres, actress and comedian*

"It isn't necessary to know exactly how your ideal life will look; you only have to know what feels better and what feels worse . . . Begin making choices based on what makes you feel freer and happier, rather than on how you think an ideal life should look. It's the process of feeling our way toward happiness, not the realization of some Platonic ideal, that creates our best lives." —*Martha Beck, life coach*

"What is passion? It is surely the becoming of a person." —*John Boorman, film director*

"Compliments are clues to your ideal style. If your coworkers say, 'That's a great color on you,' or 'Have you lost weight?' pay attention to what you're wearing and do it again. And again." —*Adam Glassman, creative director*

"I guarantee that as the balance on your outstanding loans decreases, your self-esteem will rise." —*Suze Orman, finance expert*

"You define your own life. Don't let other people write your script." —*Oprah*

"My punctuation was always kind of eccentric. I would say to my teacher, 'Well, you know, William Faulkner—he doesn't use proper punctuation.' And one of my teachers ended up devising a system with two grades, where you were graded on content and then whether it was properly written . . . Actually, [William Faulkner] is the reason I ended up passing high-school English." —*Julia Roberts, actress*

"I am not the only one failing to live up to my ludicrous expectations of myself; we all are. So maybe we all should relax." —*Lisa Wolfe, writer*

"I'd forgotten how hard it was, to *act*, to leave the self behind and become another self . . . I've worked so hard to become the woman I've become, and my hold on my identity—even after all these years—is so tenuous, I can't afford to leave my true self behind. Not even for a minute. Not even for a thousand dollars." —*Dani Shapiro, writer*

"Resolutions are like teenage hearts: they get broken an awful lot." —*Mehmet Oz, heart surgeon*

"I said to myself, I have things in my head that are not like what anyone has taught me—shapes and ideas so near to me—so natural to my way of being and thinking that it hasn't occurred to me to put them down. I decided to start anew, to strip away what I had been taught." —*Georgia O'Keeffe, artist*

"You become what you believe—not what you wish or want, but what you truly believe." —*Oprah*

"Instead of thinking, *I've failed over and over again, why bother trying again?*, take your relapse in stride and stay positive no matter how many attempts it takes you. Each new effort brings you closer to the one that might really work." —*Bob Greene, fitness trainer*

"We're all divine, but I was the only one who had the nerve to call myself that. And I thought of it first. So there!" —*Bette Midler, actress*

"When I was young, I thought confidence could be earned with perfection. Now I know that you don't earn it; you claim it. And you do that by loving the wacky, endlessly optimistic, enthusiastically uninhibited free spirit that is the essence of style, the quintessence of heart, and uniquely you." —*Cecelie Berry, writer*

"I've found that people never change behaviors in a meaningful way when the change arises from self-judgment."
—*Tara Brach, psychologist*

"To have work one loves, and a lover with whom one can work, is the longing of most women." —*Alice Walker, author and Pulitzer Prize recipient*

✳

"TAKE A LOOK AT HOW YOU MAY BE LIMITING YOUR LIFE WITH SELF-IMPOSED BOXES. WE'VE ALL DONE IT: WE MARK OUR BOXES MALE, FEMALE, WHITE, HISPANIC, AMERICAN. WE HAVE BOXES FOR HOW THIN WE ARE—OR AREN'T—AND HOW MUCH MONEY WE MAKE. WE HAVE BOXES MARKED FOR OUR PROFESSIONS AND WHERE WE LIVE . . . I HAVE CREATED A LIFE BY STEPPING OUT OF THE BOX OF PEOPLE'S LIMITATIONS. I CALL IT ZIGGING WHEN OTHERS ARE ZAGGING." —OPRAH